PRAISE FOR *WHY DIDN'T THEY HEAR US?*

"First, let me say, bravo to the author for having written this book. Obviously, this was a huge undertaking; however, she made it very clear and easy to understand all the associated issues. Secondly, I applaud her efforts to bring children's voices to light. This is such an amazing cause, often overlooked or misunderstood."
—Donna Sager Cowan, Children's Author, Speaker, Inspirer; Creator
of *the Superhero School series;* Author of *With the Courage of a Mouse* and *With the Curiosity of a Cat*

"Explore the world of overlooked, misunderstood and unheard children in this book written by Pam Orgeron, a former student of mine, who understands personally what it is to be unheard, and unappreciated. Learn about the system that has failed so many children and the ways in which these damaged souls can be healed."
—Sandra K. Henry (Thompson), Retired English Teacher, Fairview
High School, Ashland, KY

"Just reading the acknowledgment and introduction to *Why Didn't They Hear Us?* was intriguing and inspirational. Right away I wanted to read more and many of my patients came to mind that could benefit and most importantly receive healing just knowing they are not alone with not being heard as a child. After reading the rest I believe there is much healing and encouragement to be found by all who will take the time to read this book. I will be recommending this as a must-read for many of the people who come to me for help."
—Eugene (Gene) H. Benedict, M.A., LPC-S, San Antonio, Texas

WHY DIDN'T THEY HEAR US?

The Causes, Consequences, and Solutions to Children Feeling Unheard

OTHER BOOKS BY PAMELA K. ORGERON:

The ABC's of Life for Children and Adults: Short Stories, Essays, and Poems Promoting Christian Concepts (Xulon Press, 2003)

The New ABC's of Life for Children and Adults: Short Stories, Essays, and Poems Promoting Christian Concepts (ABC's Ministries, 2016)

We Survived Sexual Abuse! You Can Too! Personal Stories of Sexual Abuse Survivors with Information about Sexual Abuse Prevention, Effects, and Recovery (ABC's Ministries, 2016)

Food as an Idol: Finding Freedom from Disordered Eating (ABC's Ministries, 2017)

A Legacy to Remember: "Recollections of a Common Man" (ABC's Ministries, 2018)

Food as an Idol: The Types, Causes, Consequences, Conquering, and Prevention of Disordered Eating (ABC's Ministries, 2019)

* * *

WHY DIDN'T THEY HEAR US?

The Causes, Consequences, and Solutions to Children Feeling Unheard

Written by:
Pamela K. Orgeron, M.A., Ed.S., BCCC, ACLC
General Partner, ABC's Ministries
Nashville, TN

⅄AUTHOR ACADEMY elite

"…'Let the little children come to Me, and do not forbid them; for of such is the kingdom of God" (Mark 10:14, NKJV).

Dedication

FOR THE CHILDREN . . .

THOSE ABUSED AND BROKEN
WITHOUT A VOICE

TABLE OF CONTENTS

Appendixes

NOTE TO THE READER

As a child, I recall often feeling unheard and unappreciated by others around me. On a few occasions I even heard the statement, "Children are to be seen, and not heard". I used to think my experience was unique. However, after recently joining an online support group I was surprised when I realized my experience is more common than should be the case.

Child victims of any type of abuse feel and often are unheard. However, I have no doubt other children also go through experiences of feeling unheard. For example, I think of a child who might want to become a doctor, lawyer, or whatever but is forced by his parents to follow in their footsteps working in a family business. What happens to such children? From my observations, many of these children grow up having low self-esteem and not liking their jobs.

What is the harm of children not being listened to by parents and other individuals in their lives? Or is there harm? Of course, there is harm! If you don't believe there is harm, then look around in society at the number of children with low self-esteem, academic problems, juvenile records, and mental and physical health problems.

I believe this problem has been getting worse with each generation to result in having a society full of parents, some with the best intentions, but unprepared to be the best parents they can be to their children; thus, repeating the cycle of raising another generation of children who feel unheard and unappreciated.

At home is not the only locale where children go unheard. Children also lack a voice in many schools, churches, and other venues in society. Even in the courts of law children's voices are often suppressed leaving children victimized by the system.

Can this cycle be stopped? By writing *Why Didn't They Hear Us? The Causes, Consequences, and Solutions to Children Feeling*

Unheard I desire to bring attention to this problem in hopes of educating society on ways to combat the problem. The content of this book will focus on children in America without voices. To look any further globally would be beyond the scope of this book and my ability to identify with different cultures.

Why my concern? Because I understand what it is like to be unheard and unappreciated for the person God made me to be. For instance, during my childhood, I commonly had those feelings at Christmas time. As a child I loved reading and never cared much for jewelry. However, what did I commonly get for Christmas? Jewelry! My mother would buy gifts that she wanted me to have, not gifts that she thought I would want and enjoy. I recall one Christmas though when my father stepped in and purchased me the books *Bambi* (Simon and Schuster, 1929) and *Heidi* (Forgotten Books, 2018) as Christmas gifts. I was elated!

Honestly, I believe the trend of parents and others in America not listening to and respecting children needs to be stopped. I don't want today's children to grow up experiencing the pain and frustration that I and those in the support group for victims of sexual abuse to which I belong have felt and sometimes still feel.

By writing *Why Didn't They Hear Us?* I am not implying that all children in the United States go unheard or that all of today's parents are unhealthy. There are many parents who grew up with healthy parenting and who have children with secure, healthy self-esteems. From these individuals, I have a lot to learn. How about you? I hope you will join me as I delve into learning more about children without a voice. I invite you to please join me as I speak up to protect and help the children without voices. Let their voices be heard!!!

Pamela K. Orgeron
January 9, 2019

ACKNOWLEDGMENTS

Special thanks go to the following individuals and groups of individuals who have been instrumental in my completing the *Children without Voices* survey and ultimately the completion of this book:

- My husband, Milton J. Orgeron, who has been with me all the way

- Lola Aagaard-Boram, Morehead State University (MSU) Professor of Education, who critiqued the *Children without Voices* survey and who has been a key encourager to me since I was a student in her class at MSU

- Participants of the *Children without Voices* survey, the book is much richer with your input. A BIG thank you to those who participated!

- Sandy Henry, former English teacher at Fairview High School, Ashland, KY, thank you for your kind remarks and encouragement all the way!

- The leaders and participants of the Author Learning Center at Westbow Press' website. While a part of this group in early 2019, many in the group helped in sharing the survey and encouraged me towards writing this book. To these individuals, I also offer a BIG thank you!

- Kim Avery and the participants of her online groups, Christ-Centered Entrepreneurs and 31 Day Prayer Challenge for Coaches & Entrepreneurs, thank you for your prayer support!

- Members of my home church, Parkway Baptist Church, Goodlettsville, TN, thank you for your prayers, friendship, and ongoing support and encouragement!

- Kary Oberbrunner and the members of his online group, Igniting Souls Tribe and other authors like myself who signed up to accept Kary's Quarantine Writing Challenge, you have made my life so much richer! Thank you!
- My late parents, Harry M. and Patricia A. Owens, who paved the way for me to become an author by encouraging me to do well academically and helping me through college

My biggest thanks go to God who ultimately healed and delivered me from the wounds of not having a voice as a child. No doubt, God provided me with the talent, skill, insight, and other resources to bring this book to fruition. I also appreciated the guidance of the Holy Spirit in writing and making decisions regarding the publication of this book.

Pamela K. Orgeron
May 3, 2020

INTRODUCTION

Wanting to include the voices of other victims in *Why Didn't They Hear Us? The Causes, Consequences, and Solutions to Children Feeling Unheard*, I decided to Google the phrase "children without a voice". Boy, did I ever get a surprise! I found articles and websites about abused and neglected children, children of divorce, children of prostitutes, and foster children. With the recent passing of legislation in the state of New York allowing abortions up to birth, I also think of aborted babies as another group of "children without a voice". As I contemplate further writing, I ask myself, am I biting off more than I can chew. Yet, after sharing the topic of this new book project on my business page at Facebook, I was encouraged as a former high school teacher, Sandy Henry, wrote an online post reply to me that said this is "a book that needs to be written".

* * *

Over a year has passed since I first Googled "children without a voice". During that time I put this book on a back burner for various reasons. One factor that caused my delay in continuing to write *Why Didn't They Hear Us* is that since I could find little research on the topic of "children without voices", I decided to do my own research. I compiled a questionnaire that I ran on the Internet using surveymonkey.com during the months of February through April last year. The 35-question instrument I compiled included demographic questions, questions seeking information about past experiences of being unheard as a child, and questions seeking preventive measures to minimize the problem of children not having a voice in the future. Participants were given the option to skip questions that they were uncomfortable answering or questions that were not applicable to them. The questionnaire entitled *Children without Voices* is included in this book as Appendix A. Respondents to the questionnaire included 42 women, nine men, and one individual who preferred not to disclose his or her sex. The age range was 25 years old to 65 plus with almost 40 percent of the respondents 55-64 years old. Data, comments and suggestions from the anonymous respondents will be noted and interspersed throughout this book.

Due to getting so few respondents to the *Children without Voices* survey I became discouraged with the thought of writing this book and moved forward to write an updated version of a previously published book, *Food as an Idol: Finding Freedom from Disordered Eating* (ABC's Ministries, 2017). After publishing the new book, *Food as an Idol: The Types, Causes, Consequences, Conquering, and Prevention of Disordered Eating* (ABC's Ministries, 2019), I remained distracted from writing *Why Didn't They Hear Us?* as I was given a glimpse into four generations of one family of the pain, anguish, and damage done when children who were not listened to grew up to not listen to their own children.

Now forced into isolation at home due to the coronavirus pandemic, rather than dwell on all the chaos and negativity going on in the outside world, I have turned the isolation into a sabbatical to continue writing this book. What better time to take advantage of the current situation to continue work on this book, especially since April is National Child Abuse Prevention Month. I would rather remain positive, productive, and pro-active for the sake of my own health and wellness rather than reacting pessimistically to the world crisis.

Why Didn't They Hear Us? is divided into three sections. The first section deals with the causes, or factors contributing to children being unheard, including parental, educational, religious, legal, and societal. Section Two discusses the consequences of children not being listened to and how they may react as a response at home, at school, and in other parts of society. Section Three offers to parents, educators, Christian leaders, legal officials, and others suggestions to minimize the pain and negative reactions of children who feel and are often unheard.

In writing *Why Didn't They Hear Us? The Causes, Consequences, and Solutions to Children Feeling Unheard* I will combine my education, research, and life experience to compile a book that will be helpful to adults in recovery from being unheard as a child and also to adults—whether parents; teachers, clinicians, or others—who work with children regularly.

Pamela K. Orgeron
April 7, 2020

ABBREVIATIONS USED IN THIS BOOK:

AACC	American Association of Christian Counselors
ACE	Adverse childhood experience
ACLC	Advanced Christian Life Coach
ACS	American College of Sexologists
APA	American Psychological Association
APSAC	American Professional Society on the Abuse of Children
BCCC	Board Certified Christian Counselor
CARM	Christian Apologetics & Research Ministry
CASA/GAL	Court Appointed Special Advocates Guardians and Litem for Children
CDC	Centers for Disease Control and Prevention
CPI	Crisis Prevention Institute
cPTSD	Complex post-traumatic stress disorder
CWAVUSA	Children Without a Voice USA
CWLA	Child Welfare League of America
d2l	Darkness to Light
GERD	Gastroesophageal reflux disease
ISSTD	International Society for the Study of Trauma & Dissociation
MFMER	Mayo Foundation for Medical Education and Research
NCTSN	National Child Traumatic Stress Network
OCD	Obsessive-compulsive disorder
PTSD	Post-traumatic stress disorder
RAINN	Rape, Abuse & Incest National Network
SEL	Social and emotional learning
TMD	Temporomandibular disorder

* * *

SECTION ONE:

Factors Contributing to Children Feeling Unheard

- Parental Factors
- Educational Factors
- Toxic Faith
- Legal Factors
- Societal Issues

CHAPTER 1

Let's Talk About Parenting!

"...I, the Lord your God, am a jealous God, [b]visiting the iniquity of the fathers upon the children to the third and fourth generations..." (Deuteronomy 5:9, NKJV).

Parenting in simplest terms refers to child rearing. A broader definition would be the processes, guidance, etc. offered to children from birth to adulthood that promotes their development, including physical, emotional, intellectual, psychological, social, and spiritual. One does not necessarily have to be a child's biological parent to parent a specific child, as many grandparents, other relatives, and other individuals (e.g.: foster parents) parent children in today's society.

Research commonly suggests four basic parenting styles:

- Permissive
- Neglectful
- Authoritarian
- Authoritative

Permissive parents, as the name would imply, typically indulge their children and offer little if any structure to allow each child to do whatever he or she wants. Neglectful parents fail to get involved in the lives of their children and communicate very little with them. Authoritarian parents could be compared to a dictator. They have rigid standards offering children no say so in what happens in the family. Often, in these homes parents have the attitude and approach with children, "It's our way or the highway". Authoritative parenting, the most advantageous to children, offers children loving limits, healthy communication, and realistic expectations. Table 1 outlines the pros, cons, and typical child outcomes for each of the four parenting styles.

TABLE 1. Parenting Styles

Parenting Style	Pros	Cons	Outcome in Child
Permissive	Parents express love.	No boundaries	Child feels loved but insecure.
Neglectful	—	*No discipline *Little love expressed	Deep emotional scars
Authoritarian	—	*Overcorrect children *Poor expression of love	Rebellious
Authoritative	*Very loving *Clear healthy boundaries	—	Well-adjusted

Does parenting style affect whether a child grows up to feel heard and understood? Of course! For example, in my own case, my parents were very authoritarian in nature. I was always told what I had to do and never taught how to make my own decisions. Strict to the core, that's how my parents were as far back as I can remember. I recall in my early years how my father often overcorrected my grammar at the dinner table making me not want to say anything. Additionally, I was never allowed to question their authority about anything. Nor did my parents give out hugs or words of affection, such as "I love you", when I was a child. I recall feeling misunderstood and unheard by my parents most of the time whenever I was a child. In the survey

Children without Voices I asked whether the participants felt listened to by their parents or other primary caregiver in their childhood. The responses of the participants are reflected in Table 2:

TABLE 2: Did you feel listened to by your parents or other primary caregiver in your childhood?

Answer Choices	Responses	Percentage
Always	4	7.69
Usually	21	40.38
Sometimes	9	17.31
Rarely	13	25.00
Never	5	9.62
TOTAL	52	

Many reasons exist why parents fail to listen to their children. Three primary reasons come to my mind: ignorance, distractions, and apathy. Let's look at each of these reasons more in depth.

Ignorance

Ignorance may be bliss in some situations but not when it comes to parenting. When parents are uneducated for whatever reason on how to listen appropriately to their children, the children suffer. When a parent has had poor role models as a child, that parent does not know how to respond to children in healthy ways. As a former therapist of mine said, "Typically, parents parent in the way that they were parented themselves, unless they recognize the dysfunction in their upbringing and choose to do differently."

In the case of my parents, I believe my mother felt unheard as she was lost in the shuffle of eleven children. My father, an only child, did not have younger siblings or other relatives to watch growing up to learn how parents and children should interact in healthy ways. Had I not had other healthy family role models and learned about what entails a healthy family through my education, I too would have been doomed to repeat the pattern.

In the *Children without Voices* survey I asked whether participants thought ignorance was a cause for their feeling unheard by parents or other primary caregiver. Almost 70 percent of the 45 participants who responded to the question reported that they thought parental/ caregiver ignorance was a cause for their

> **"Typically, parents parent in the way that they were parented themselves, unless they recognize the dysfunction in their upbringing and choose to do differently."**

parents/caregiver not listening to them, at least sometimes. Less than 20 percent of the 45 respondents believed ignorance did not play a role in their not feeling unheard by their parents or other primary caregiver as a child.

Distractions

Distractions…our lives are full of them! In the *Children without Voices* survey I asked whether participants thought distractions, such as poor health or job responsibilities, were a cause for their feeling unheard by parents or other primary caregiver when they were a child. Almost 83 percent of the 47 participants who responded to the question reported distractions as a contributing factor in their parents not hearing them as a child.

What might distract a parent from listening to his or her child? Here's a list of things that I believe can come between a parent and child having a healthy relationship:

- Parent's job
- Caring for aging parents
- Other children
- Health issues, whether physical or mental
- Misplaced priorities

Can you think of others? No doubt, my list is not exhaustive.

In my family, my mother failed to listen to me a lot due to her obsession with having to keep a "spotless" house. It seemed to me she would rather clean the house than interact with me. Dad seemed to listen more but was often distracted by caring for his aging mother, a widow; by caring for my mentally ill mother; or, by pressures and responsibilities related to providing for our family.

Apathy

Let's get real! There are just some people out there who are indifferent or do not care to have a relationship with their children, which I would equate to being selfish. In the *Children without Voices* survey I asked whether participants thought selfishness was a cause for their feeling unheard by parents or other primary caregiver when they were a child. Less than 24 percent of the 46 individuals who responded to the question reported selfishness was never a cause for their being unheard by a parent or guardian as a child. On a personal note, I think of one instance where an individual cared more about getting access to drugs rather than treating his child in an appropriate manner. As the story was told to me, this man obviously cared more about getting drugs than treating his child appropriately.

I believe some parents learn apathy from their own parents or other poor role models. In some cases, I might equate apathy to *learned helplessness*. Learned helplessness, as the phrase might suggest, is where a child grows up and fails to take responsibility in life. For example, I think of a child who is always told by a parent that he or she will never be anybody. After being told that one will never be anybody repeatedly over a period of years, the child will begin to believe that he or she is helpless; thus, neglecting to become a responsible adult. It in essence becomes a *self-fulfilled prophecy*.

In conclusion, regardless of the reasons why a parent does not hear his or her child, that child will more than likely suffer negative effects, which will be discussed in Section 2, Chapter 6.

* * *

CHAPTER 2

The Unheard Child at School

In the *Children without Voices* survey I asked two distinct questions regarding school. First, I asked whether participants felt they were listened to by teachers. Then I asked whether they felt heard by their peers or classmates. The responses of the participants are reflected in Table 3 and Table 4:

TABLE 3: Did you feel listened to by your teachers?

Answer Choices	Responses	Percentage
Always	2	3.85
Usually	25	48.08
Sometimes	17	32.69
Rarely	6	11.54
Never	2	3.85
TOTAL	52	

TABLE 4: Did you feel listened to by your peers/classmates?

Answer Choices	Responses	Percentage
Always	2	3.85
Usually	23	44.23
Sometimes	14	26.92
Rarely	10	19.23
Never	3	5.77
TOTAL	52	

What might contribute to a child not feeling heard and understood at school? Here's what comes to my mind:

- Unsupportive teachers and/or other school officials
- Competition with other students for the teacher's attention
- Bullying from other students

Unsupportive Teachers and/or other School Officials

Regardless of whether intentional, let's face the truth that there are some teachers and school officials who do not listen to students. For example, I think of the burned out teacher or school administrator who is only working his or her position for the money and has become apathetic to the needs of the children. Another example might be the teacher or administrator who is so distracted by family problems at home that he or she does not have the energy or focus required to pay attention to students.

Fear also may play a big factor as to why teachers and other school officials do not listen and come to the aid of children, especially those children who are being abused at home. In the article "Why the Cry of the Beaten Child Goes Unheard", Beckelman reported what one fourth-grade teacher said.

A mother told me in confidence that her husband was beating their son. She made me promise not to say anything because she was afraid of ruining the marriage. But the kid was a real behavior problem. I was afraid to report it because, if I broke her confidence, I'd sever the only link I had with the family. I also feared that the father would retaliate by beating the kid even more. I talked to our school psychologist who agreed that I should continue trying to work through the mother. He also suggested that I pray and use lots of Band-Aids with Vaseline.[1]

Beckelman went on to share the account of another teacher who feared retribution from a father suspected of abusing one of her students.

One teacher relates a meeting she had with her principal and the father of a child she suspected was abused. She felt that the father was "glaring" at her throughout the meeting. For days afterward, she had a friend pick her up at school rather than travel home alone.[2]

In today's society teachers and administrators face a strong demand on their time that would be better devoted to listening to children. Instead, teachers and administrators must devote excessive time to record keeping. Furthermore, classrooms can be overcrowded where teachers do not have adequate time and energy to devote to individual students.

Cultural differences also may play a factor in whether a child feels heard and understood by teachers and other school officials. For example, in some cultures children are taught that it is more respectful to stay quiet and not initiate conversations with adults. If the teacher is not aware of this cultural difference, he or she may think a child understands something clearly when in reality the child is confused.

Not only can cultural differences affect whether a child feels heard by a teacher or other school official, but language barriers between the student and adult may hinder understanding between the two individuals. As a side note, since I believe America was founded as an English speaking country, I believe English should be the standard language taught in every school. This should help minimize language barriers between students and school faculty.

Competition with other Students for the Teacher's Attention

Competition is the name of the game in today's world. The classroom setting and other school environments are no different. Star athletes and high achieving students naturally attract the listening ears of teachers and other school officials. I know that from personal experience. As a high achieving student, I almost always felt listened to by my teachers and other school officials. On the other hand, I doubt that the average Joe or Sally felt heard much? How does he or she compete to be heard in the classroom?

Students who have parents involved in school activities also may be more likely to be heard by teachers and other school officials. In such cases, the parents may become the voice of the child creating less of a need for the child to interact with school officials.

Unless teachers and other school employees are intentional about developing individual relationships with ALL students, some students may interpret their lack of engagement as not listening or caring about their needs. Personal biases, or favoritism, should never be the motive for teachers and other school officials listening to children in school.

Bullying from other Students

To one degree or another, I do not believe that there has ever been a child in any school who has not been bullied about something by another student. Of course, attitudes and behaviors towards bullies have changed since I was in school in the 1960s and 70s. Looking back, I was bullied by other students for being heavier than other girls in my class. I also was teased, and made fun of for being a high achiever academically. It wasn't called bullying then but was simply considered teasing or being made fun of. Most students in my generation who were bullied simply ignored the bullies or played on their strong points (e.g. athletic ability) to be heard by others.

In my opinion I believe both bullies and the students they bully go unheard but in different ways. The bullies, I believe, bully because they feel unheard in at least one area of their life (e.g., at home; the abused or neglected child) and act out through bullying as a means to get attention, perhaps as a "cry for help". Those who are the targets of bullies more than likely, as I did as a child, feel unheard and misunderstood by the bullies. I remember when I was bullied for being a "Miss Goody Two Shoes". In hindsight, I must have thought *if you only knew the wrath at home that I would have to go through if I got into trouble drinking, doing drugs, or anything else considered bad or sinful.*

Before closing this chapter I want to point out two key points I believe to be true. First of all, I do not believe students today who are bullied have the resilience or the know how to brush off harsh comments from other students like those in my generation could do. Secondly, bullies today seem meaner and have more means of bullying others through the various social websites on the Internet, such as Facebook. In today's world, bullying is a more serious issue that can end in tragedy. The consequences of bullying at school will be discussed in Section 2, Chapter 7.

* * *

CHAPTER 3

Children Silenced by Toxic Faith

Though our Heavenly Father hears all the cries of His children, not all children feel heard in places of worship or by those claiming to be a part of God's family. What might contribute to this occurring? I suggest four primary reasons:

- False prophets
- Church cliques
- Church bullies
- Individual factors

False Prophets

Just as the controlling authoritarian parent likes to rule the home, I have heard of pastors who rule their congregations with an iron fist. These so called men of God always get the final word, perhaps not even seeking advice or listening to the needs of his congregation or followers, which include children.

In churches where toxic faith exists children are expected to fit into a mold of what the pastor deems appropriate behavior for children. Child expectations may be passed down from the pastor through other church leaders or parents. I think "aloof" pastors who operate this way might leave a child feeling as if the pastor is unapproachable and that he doesn't care enough to listen to him or her. On the other hand, a child may put these pastors or false prophets on a pedestal as if they could do no wrong.

How can a person recognize these false prophets? Thom S. Rainer, founder and CEO of Church Answers, suggests fourteen indicators that a person is ungodly and toxic to the faith.[3] Summarized, they are:

- Lack fruit of the Spirit (Galatians 5:22-23)
- Minimum accountability partners; autocratic in nature
- Different standards of behavior for self and others
- Feel superior to others; critical of others to build up self
- Show favoritism
- Defensive when disagreed with.
- They have a forked tongue.
- They try to write people off before helping them. "People are means to their ends; they see them as projects, not God's people who need mentoring and developing."[4]
- Manipulative
- Lack openness
- Does not allow others to have different opinions
- Surround themselves with flatterers and "yes people"
- Poor communicators
- Self-centered

In addition to the unhealthy characteristics offered by Rainer, I also think of those false prophets who actively prey on children. The perfect example would be the sexual abuse scandal in the Catholic Church. I too was a victim of abuse from a man whom others claim carried the message of the Gospel at one point in his life. Such cases are often covered up never giving the child a voice to heal from the wounds of the perpetrator.

Another scenario in churches where a child might not have a voice is where a church has a "senior" mentality. By this I mean that the church members consist mainly of senior citizens who really do not care much about being around young people. I know about one church where a lot of the members had this mindset. The church offered few activities for children and was at a stalemate in terms of church growth.

No offense against anyone in the church I grew up attending as a child but honestly, I did not feel that the children had any voice there. The church had no Sunday school or activities for youth. Furthermore, according to my mother, the church body overall did not believe that a child could be saved. This belief contradicts Jesus' approach to children:

> [13] *Then they brought little children to Him, that He might touch them; but the disciples rebuked those who brought them.* [14] *But when Jesus saw it, He was greatly displeased and said to them, "Let the little children come to Me, and do not forbid them; for of such is the kingdom of God.* [15] *Assuredly, I say to you, whoever does not receive the kingdom of God as a little child will by no means enter it."* [16] *And He took them up in His arms, laid His hands on them, and blessed them*
> (Mark 10:13-16, NKJV).

Church Cliques

Similar to how there are cliques in schools, in my experience more often than not churches too have cliques that fail to give a voice to outsiders, including children. Often I have seen churches where most of the leadership team was all members of one particular extended family. I know of one case where a person grew up in a church where members of one or two families filled all the key leadership positions. As a child, that person felt inferior and sometimes snubbed by children who came from the "ruling" families.

Church Bullies

Just as there are bullies in educational settings, such as schools, churches too have their bullies. I would equate the toxic spiritual leader as a bully but there can be others. One mother reported,

"Things can get out of hand at church just as easily as they do at school. (I found my son locked in a closet one night at youth group.) It's tragic when bullying shows up at church."[5]

Individual Factors

Aside from false prophets, church cliques, and church bullies, children possess individual attributes that influence whether they feel heard and understood in church settings. What are these attributes?

- A child's level of resiliency
- A child's family support
- Any health issue, whether mental or physical
- The child's temperament/personality

Resiliency. What is resilience? Dent and Cameron (2003) defined resilience:

Resilience is the concept that is used to describe the flexibility that allows certain children to cope with and manage major difficulties and disadvantages in life, and even to thrive in the face of what appear to be overwhelming odds (p.5).[6]

Family support. The amount and type of family support a child has may influence whether that child is heard and understood in Christian circles. For example, in my experience most children of parents who are active in ministry at a particular church get more attention and more of a voice than the "latch-key" children who may be bused in to the church without parental support. This should not be the case but I have seen it happen.

Health issues. Health issues, and not always the health issues of the child, may affect whether a child is given a voice at a church. For example, perhaps there is a disabled child in the family who has a lot of needs and the congregation gives the disabled child more attention than the healthy one. Or, on the other hand, the situation may play out with the opposite scenario where the handicapped, disabled child is neglected and the healthy child gets all the attention.

Child's temperament and/or personality. Personally, I think how good of a fit that a child's personality is with the personality of the church also would affect whether a child feels heard and understood. For example, a quiet, shy child by nature might feel very uncomfortable and unheard thrown into the midst of a large, charismatic congregation. The quiet, shy child might feel more comfortable in a more reserved congregation that is less expressive.

In closing, in this chapter primarily I imply "church" as meaning a building where individuals go to worship. However, most in the faith understand the church to refer to the members of the body of Christ, not the building. Regardless of the meaning one applies to the term "church", whether as a building or the body of Christians, when children have no voice in the church damage can occur. That damage will be discussed in Section 2, Chapter 8.

* * *

CHAPTER 4

Child Victims Silenced by "The System"

This chapter is very personal to me, as I write from three unique perspectives: 1. from the perspective of a former child victim whom the system failed greatly, 2. from the perspectives of being a mandated reporter as a Board Certified Christian Counselor (BCCC) and a Board Certified Advanced Christian Life Coach (ACLC), and 3. from the perspective of being a former foster mother. Though I know a lot of children have been helped through social services and the legal system, I know a lot of situations where the system has failed children. I was one of those children whom the legal system failed.

My Story

To protect the innocent, I won't be going into detail sharing specific information about other victims involved, etc. What I will share about is how my voice was silenced and some unfair principles I have had to accept and face in my recovery from what happened.

To summarize what happened, at the age of about 4 years old I was a key witness who wanted to testify to a horrendous crime that was covered up by relatives, crooked lawyers, and others who were bought off to silence my voice and the voices of other children who witnessed the crime and who also wanted to testify. How did this happen?

"You're too young." Taught by my paternal grandmother that honesty is always the best policy, I wanted and was determined to testify and tell the truth. However, I wasn't permitted to because people said, "She's too young. She doesn't know what she is talking about."

About the other children and me who witnessed the crime, other people said, "They're so young. They'll forget about what happened. It would be their word against his word. Who would believe the children?" Thus, the voices of the children involved were silenced for decades until as an adult I recalled the memories and was able to share the truth, which set me free from years of anxiety, PTSD, and other emotional and psychological wounds that resulted from all the pent-up pain and anger from what happened.

Money talks. Unfortunately, the young ages of the other children involved and myself were not the only factors that contributed to us children's voices being shut down. The perpetrator had contacts with wealthy individuals who paid off the local judge "to make the case go away".

Though what happened was repressed and even forgotten by some over time, I believe God always gets the last word. In Scripture we are told

> ²*For there is nothing covered that will not be revealed, nor hidden that will not be known.* ³ *Therefore whatever you have spoken in the dark will be heard in the light, and what you have spoken in the ear in inner rooms will be proclaimed on the housetops* (Luke 12:2-3, NKJV).

Yes, my voice was silenced for decades but eventually the truth comes out.

Though what happened was repressed and even forgotten by some over time, I believe God always gets the last word.

A Mandated Reporter

Even before I became a BCCC, which first established me as a mandated reporter, I always strived to live by my paternal grandmother's adage, "Honesty is always the best policy". Additionally, I always had a big heart for children and hated to see one who was hurting. Thus, I did not fail to speak out for children in harm's way. For example, years before I started graduate school or had even thought about going into counseling, I recall having babysat with a young girl who shared with me that she had been sexually molested at a local daycare center. What did I do? I went straight to a friend who was a police officer and filed a report. After an investigation followed, the day care center was shut down. In that particular case, I was glad that I was able to speak out and be the voice for that helpless little girl.

As a BCCC and as an ACLC, I take my professional ethics as a mandated reporter very seriously. As difficult as the situation was, I have even turned in friends anonymously who were covering up abuse in their own families. I always stand for the truth and advocate for children.

Foster Parenting

Based on research[7] and my personal experience as a foster mother, I firmly believe that the system fails children far too often. In 1993, Stacy Robinson, a third-year student at the Emory School of Law, Atlanta, Georgia wrote the following:

> *The role of protecting a minor falls upon the parents as natural guardians first. In cases of abuse and neglect, however, where a parent has failed to protect the child, the state steps in as parens patriae. This often means moving the child from the home and placing the child in foster care. Unfortunately, under the current foster care system, the state often fails to protect the child from harm and may even add to the harm suffered.*[8]

Though Robinson wrote the aforementioned quote over 25 years ago, I believe the general premise is still true in today's world.

In 1978 Laurie Beckelman reported in an article in *The New York Times* about how a lack of follow up to reported cases of child abuse was widespread mainly from a lack of funding and sufficient staff. Beckelman wrote,

> *The average caseworker handles a load of 20 to 25 cases and cannot cope with them all. The pressure is often so overwhelming that turnover rates are high, and families don't receive the consistent care and support they need. According to Douglas Besharov, director of H.E.W.'s National Center on Child Abuse and Neglect in Washington—which helps support state programs and has assisted in developing the new service techniques—this is true of most communities in the country. Though still only 30 percent of all suspected child-abuse cases are ever reported, this is a dramatic increase over the number reported 10 years ago. Funding, training, and supervision have not kept up with demand for services*[9].

Based on complaints from employees within the foster care system who worked with my husband and me a few years back, the situation hasn't changed much since 1978. We were told of how counselors and social workers within the system frequently burnout leaving those who remain employed overworked and not able to give the individual attention that each child needs.

More recently, in 2019 Sankaran wrote about the case of a 16 year old client in foster care who wanted to go before a judge to tell her story but was denied repeatedly.

> *The old English proverb states "children should be seen and not heard." My case illustrates how the foster care system often takes this one step further–it asks that children both be unseen and unheard. A national survey of youth in foster care found that less than 15 percent had attended most court hearings. A third had never even attended a single hearing in*

their case. Chances are if you head to a juvenile court in most parts of the country, you won't see a kid there.[10]

What happens to children whose voices go unacknowledged by the system? The answer to that question will be discussed in Section 2, Chapter 9.

* * *

CHAPTER 5

Societal Taboos...False Beliefs Wreaking Havoc in Children's Lives

"A fundamental barrier confronting the would-be intervener is the fact that society doesn't really support intervention."[11]

If you felt unheard by society as a child, you are not alone. Most of the participants in the *Children without Voices* survey reported feeling the same way. See Table 5.

TABLE 5: As a child, did you feel listened to in society (church, government, etc.), in general?

Answer Choices	Responses	Percentage
Always	1	1.92
Usually	10	19.23
Sometimes	14	26.92
Rarely	21	40.38
Never	6	11.54
TOTAL	52	

Why would so many people have felt unheard in society as a child? I propose that false beliefs are a major contributing factor to this problem. Everyone has false beliefs that they were taught or developed unconsciously as a child. I was no exception to this reality. In this chapter I will discuss false beliefs I recognize and some I have even struggled with to overcome.

"Family Secrets" are Okay

Society is full of clichés that support this false belief. From "a man's home is his castle" to what I was told as a child, "What happens in this family stays in this family". When discussing with one individual the unhealthiness of family secrets, the remark was made, "That's my private business".

The individual who remarked about his "private business" is one of four generations in a family line where people have attempted to cover up child abuse or neglect that has been passed down through generations. From my perspective, the dysfunction

> **Whether the motive for an outsider's not reporting is due to fear of retribution or just not wanting to get involved, whatever the situation, I believe this further robs an abused child of his right to be heard and to get needed help.**

has grown progressively worse with each generation to the point where the youngest person in the family line is in state custody.

In my opinion, believing that family secrets are okay is detrimental to a child's voice being heard in two ways. First, when an abused child hears "don't talk" enough, that child may become too fearful to reach out to others outside the family to get help. The child's pain becomes buried to manifest years later in the form of emotional and psychological problems, as was the situation in my own life. I lived in denial from childhood abuse until depression, anxiety, and PTSD surfaced forcing me to take my voice back and allowing me to share my story with others as an adult.

The second way that the stigma of protecting family secrets is harmful is when family outsiders know about or suspect abuse but then fail to report. Whether the motive for an outsider's not reporting is due to fear of retribution or just not wanting to get involved, whatever the situation, I believe this further robs an abused child of his right to be heard and to get needed help. In my own family, I know several extended family members knew of the abuse going on in my immediate family but failed to confront the situation due to various reasons. For my paternal grandmother, she told me that she said nothing because of her fear that we children would be put in foster care where she would never be able to see us again.

"Children Are to be Seen, and Not Heard"

What is the meaning of this statement? *Writing Explained*, a phrase and idiom dictionary shares the following definition:

> *Children can be present in a conversation but should not speak, particularly when they are around adults.*
> *Unlike many idioms in English the meaning of this proverb is literal. This proverb stems back to the religious views of medieval culture. The initial meaning of this proverb was that young women should not speak in the presence of adults but later evolved to include all children.*[12]

Dr. Lanae St.John, ACS, a board certified sexologist with the American College of Sexologists (ACS) and an Intimacy & Relationship Coach, pointed out the following in a blog article entitled "Why Raising Children To Be 'Seen And Not Heard' Makes Them Targets For Predators":

> *This phrase suggests that little boys and girls should be well-behaved and keep quiet. Often girls are socialized to be much more submissive and quiet than boys, but I know this phrase impacts boys as well.*
> *The phrase was applied to me mostly when I would run around like a loud, obnoxious little kid and someone wanted me to stop doing that. It worked eventually, I guess, from an exhausted and tired parent's perspective. My spirit was "broken" and I became the typical first born who never breaks any of the rules my parents set for me.*[13]

Much like Dr. St.John after being told "Children are to be seen and not heard" I too, more often than not, became one of those compliant well-behaved children who dared not question the authority of my parents.

Fighting is a Good Way to Resolve Conflict

The individual mentioned previously who referred to family secrets as his private business, also bought into the notion that fighting was the answer to any disagreement. A common statement out of his mouth when confronted with something he disagreed with was "Let's take it outside". By that, he meant do you want to fight it out. Fighting had become his means for dealing with conflict growing up.

When children buy into this "let's take it outside" mindset, whether the conflict is with another child or an adult, healthy communication cannot exist. Neither party in the dispute has a voice.

Fighting is appropriate as conflict resolution only in situations of self-defense against a physical attack, and even then the "loser" often vows later to settle the score in their view, which simply prolongs the conflict instead of resolving it. When fighting is accepted as a way to resolve ordinary conflict, the wrong lesson is taught, that "might makes right". So whoever is the biggest bully determines right and wrong by whatever they want to claim for themselves or whoever they want to dominate, regardless of any objective standards of right and wrong. If the whole society were allowed to be run this way, the result would be violent chaos. So neither should "might makes right" be allowed to be the ruling principle in families or other parts of society.

Sticks and Stones May Break my Bones, but Words Can Never Hurt Me

"Sticks and stones may break my bones but names will never hurt me" is a stock response to verbal bullying in school play-grounds throughout the English-speaking world. It sounds a little antiquated these days and has no doubt been superseded by more streetwise comebacks.[14].

In grade school I recall not being able to do cartwheels like most of the other girls in my class. Naturally, I was hurt when my classmates teased me about this inability of mine. Whenever I shared my feelings at home about the situation, I was told of the sticks and stones reply to make, which my parents hoped would silence the voices of my critics. In hindsight, my parents invalidated my voice.

Let's Take God out of America!

Though I don't recall anyone in my circle of influence as a child ever shouting "Let's take God out of America!" the world around us has seemed to scream that message over the years. If you don't believe me, take a look at how prayer has been taken out of our schools since I was a child. I recall having been an active member of my school's prayer group growing up. Now short of being in a Christian school, most schools today forbid such assemblies of students. Aside from the false beliefs discussed previously in this chapter, I believe the greatest reason children do not have a voice in society is because we, as a society, have fallen away from God and do not see children through God's eyes.

* * *

"If My people who are called by My name will humble themselves, and pray and seek My face, and turn from their wicked ways, then I will hear from heaven, and will forgive their sin and heal their land" (2 Chronicles 7:14, NKJV).

SECTION TWO:

Consequences of Children Feeling Unheard

- At Home
- At School
- In the Church
- In the Courts
- In Society

CHAPTER 6

When Children Go Unheard in the Home, What Happens?

Both children and parents can suffer, I believe, when the voices of children go unheard in the home. First, let's look at the reactions of children who feel unheard and misunderstood in the home.

Children without a Voice in the Home

The responses to children not having a voice in the home can vary depending upon a child's personality, culture, and other factors. Children may react to not being given a voice in the home with anger and vindictiveness, with quiet complacency, or with honesty (it is what it is). There may be anger at the parents or others in the home who fail to listen to a child. This anger may become self-directed where the child feels used and discarded, having images of being unattractive and unwanted that can result in depression, anxiety, and/ or eating disorders.

"Forms of quiet complacency include denial, rationalization, and 'forgive and forget' without facing reality. Many persons who are sexually abused in early childhood will tend to make excuses for the perpetrator or minimize the damage."[15]

Though there are other reasons besides being sexually abused that a child may not have a voice in a home, I believe that regardless of the reason, the long term effects of being unheard could be similar to those in an untreated sexually abused child. The long term effects of untreated childhood sexual abuse may include:

- *PTSD and/or anxiety*
- *Depression and thoughts of suicide*
- *Sexual anxiety and disorders, including promiscuity*
- *Difficulty maintaining appropriate boundaries with others, including enmeshed or avoidant relationships*
- *Poor body image and low self-esteem*
- *The use of unhealthy behaviors, such as alcohol abuse, drug abuse, self-mutilation, or bingeing and purging, to help mask painful emotions related to the abuse.*[16]

Previously I have discussed how I felt that I had no voice as a child in our home. What was my response? In hindsight, where I didn't get the positive attention at home that I craved, I subconsciously sought attention from teachers and others outside the home through being a high-achieving student. Furthermore, to me it seemed that the only time I was heard at home was when I did something bad or did not perform to my parents' expectations.

Doing something bad always resulted in the kind of attention I didn't want (e.g.: a spanking). To avoid the discipline, I became a compliant, model child, at least, according to some of my aunts who said I was the model child, in comparison to other children they knew. My mom, at least, did not agree with my aunts. My father too had his moments of being critical. I recall those times when I would bring home a report card that wasn't straight A's. I never heard, "That's a great report card!" What I heard was "Why isn't that 'B' an 'A'?"

> **I never heard, "That's a great report card!" What I heard was "Why isn't that 'B' an 'A'?"**

I never felt that I measured up to my parents' expectations. I became very perfectionistic with a low self-esteem. I felt powerless, betrayed, and ashamed of the situation at home, my mother being mentally ill. I also experienced a lot of *cognitive dissonance* about future expectations. At one time, I might have high hopes of going to college and making a better life for myself. On the other hand, at another time, I recall telling my locker partner how I did not want to live. She replied, "You won't kill yourself because you still have dreams." I thank God she was right at that time; although, years later as an adult going through depression, I did attempt suicide twice unsuccessfully.

The Losses of Parents Who Don't Listen

Though I believe children experience the greatest loss when parents fail to listen to them, parents too can be at a great loss. What might some of those losses be?

- Loss of child's respect
- Loss of child's trust
- Poorer communication with child
- Loss of child's interest in relating to parent
- Child grows up estranged from parent

The losses I propose are based on what I know at least one of my parents experienced from my not being listened to as a child. To be honest, though I toed the line in terms of behaving most of the time, I did not feel respected by my mother so I didn't have much respect for her until later in my adult years.

Trust also is important in a parent child relationship. My mother did not give me a whole lot as a child to make me want to trust her when I was growing up. Although, in hindsight now, I realize her not listening to me was not intentional but was due to the mental illness that she struggled with all her life.

With not much respect or trust between my mother and me growing up, it stands to reason that we did not communicate very well. I preferred to stay in my room studying because it always seemed that whenever my mother did have something to say to me it was always negative and critical, which usually ended up with us in a screaming match, especially during my teen years.

My mother never felt the joy of having a healthy relationship with me growing up like many of my school girlfriends' mothers had with them. I attribute that to the fact that because she wasn't interested in getting to know the real me, I had no interest in relating to her until later after I became an adult.

Although, I wouldn't say that I grew up estranged from my mother, our relationship was quite strained. Furthermore, it was non-existent for a long time when I was a young adult going through psychotherapy to heal from the abuse in my past. After I went through therapy and began to see my mother through God's eyes and had a better perspective of why she had behaved as she did when I was growing up, our relationship improved immensely. In fact, months before Mom died she apologized to me about how I had been hurt as a child. In the end, my husband and I were blessed to be with Mom as she took her last breath here on earth to enter Glory.

In regards to my father's losses of those times I felt he didn't listen or understand me, such as when he was critical of my grades, he missed out on the joy of celebrating all the A's I had received. Honestly, I always was known as a "daddy's girl" growing up so I have little to fault my father about. At the orders of my therapist my father's and my relationship, like my mother's and my relationship, was non-existent whenever I was in recovery.

The only other thing that my father did that really hurt and bothered me was whenever he would be critical of my weight. In hindsight, his comments about my weight may have been a catalyst in setting me up for the eating disorder that I struggled with and overcame as a young adult.

In concluding this chapter, I want to say that in hindsight I believe both my parents did the best they knew to do with the light and resources that they were given. I am most grateful and feel blessed to have had them as my parents.

* * *

CHAPTER 7

What Happens to Children Silenced at School?

In Chapter 2 we looked at how unsupportive teachers and/or other school officials, how competition among students for the teacher's attention, and how bullying from other students can play a role in a child not feeling heard or understood in educational settings. In this chapter the consequences of students being unheard in the classroom will be discussed.

When Teachers and Administrators Don't Listen

Similar to how a child's personality, culture, and other factors affect the reactions of children whose parents do not listen to them, I believe there are factors that can create a diversity of responses to when teachers and administrators do not listen to children. Factors that come to my mind include:

- Support of parents or other caretakers in the child's life
- Support of friends
- Child's Intelligence
- Child's personality or disposition

Parental support. Whether a child's parents or other caregivers support and encourage that child to learn and do well at school can go a long way in influencing a child, regardless of whether teachers or administrators listen to the child. I know this is true because I remember in grade school when I had a teacher whom I felt did not like me because she seemed to show favoritism to other students in the class. When I voiced this concern to family members, they encouraged me to not let the teacher's actions bother me and to work hard doing well in the class anyway.

Other students at my school growing up had little encouragement from home to do well academically. Often when these students went unheard by teachers and administrators, these students only became more despondent and destitute not doing well in their classwork. For example, I know of one family where the father was an alcoholic who wasted all his money on booze. The behaviors of his children as students seemed to lie on opposite ends of a continuum. One daughter was very well-behaved, quiet and shy, as if to not draw anyone's attention. The boys in the family took to the opposite extreme, always acting out and staying in trouble to get attention.

Support of friends. "Birds of a feather flock together." This is true of students in educational settings too. Whether a child chooses to have friends and the type of friends a child chooses to have at school can either support or offset the negative effects that might result when teachers and administrators fail to listen to a particular child. In my case, I recall how hanging out with the "brains" of the class always motivated me to work harder to make the grade, regardless of whether I felt the teacher liked me or whether I liked the teacher, and, believe me, I had more than one teacher who was not to my liking.

Child's intelligence. Similar to how parental support and the support of friends can either support or offset the negative effects that might result when teachers and administrators do not listen to a particular child, I believe that a child's intelligence level can either make or break the success of that child in the classroom. For example, a more intelligent child may realize that a teacher's indifference to him or her has nothing to do with the child but realizes the teacher may be distracted by other problems. As a result, the child may not be affected negatively by a teacher's not listening to him or her.

Child's personality or disposition. According to Timothy A. Pychyl, Ph.D., who conducted a study exploring the relationship between personality and academic achievement, "previous research indicates that the personality trait of conscientiousness is the strongest personality predictor of academic performance (as important as cognitive ability in terms of prediction)".[17] Given that information, I would think that the more conscientious, or self-motivated student, would be less disturbed by a teacher's inattentiveness.

Pros and Cons to Competition in the Classroom

In my experience, I believe, competition in the classroom can be healthy or unhealthy. When a student is motivated to learn and is challenged to compete against self rather than competing against others I believe competition can be healthy. Why do I think this? First, you must know that I have always had a competitive nature and I still do. Ask my husband.

At my high school awards were always given out every year to the most outstanding student in each class. At the end of my freshman year, ending the year with a straight "A" average, I only received one of those rewards. I should have been satisfied with that but when my classmates rubbed it in about awards they received that I didn't get, I got mad and jealous, determined to show

> **When a student is motivated to learn and is challenged to compete against self rather than competing against others I believe competition can be healthy.**

my classmates the next academic year. Needless to say, I worked hard enough to receive four class awards out of the five classes I took during my sophomore year. Who was upset then? Not me, but other people complained to the administration that one child should not be permitted to receive so many awards, even though that child may have the highest percentage of all the students in that particular class, which I did.

In the above account for me to compete against myself was healthy but when I started comparing myself to the other students and what they had accomplished, that was when the competition became unhealthy. I should have been satisfied with the fact that I had ended my freshman year with straight A's and one award.

Bullying Harmful to All Students

In Chapter 2 I mentioned how bullying can end in tragedy. How so? Research[18] abounds on the negative effects of bullying at school. The APA reports how bullying and the climate at school affect the learning and development of both the children being bullied and the bully. Children bullied by others quit school more often; make lower grades; have poorer self-esteem; experience more depression, anxiety, and loneliness; and, are at greater risk for attempting suicide.

Students who bully typically are more aggressive and impulsive with more of them abusing alcohol and drugs. They also tend to be involved in antisocial and criminal behavior more.

The US government recognizes bullying as an ACE (adverse childhood experience) that can have long-term effects on physical and emotional health. The same CDC study found that even those who witness bullying are at a higher rate for alcohol and drug use, depression, sleep disturbance, heart disease, and eating disorders, creating even more unhappy youth who may lash out at others, perpetuating the cycle.[19]

In today's world, students often take bullying of other students beyond classroom walls through the use of cyberbullying, which has unique concerns.

The content an individual shares online—both their personal content as well as any negative, mean, or hurtful content— creates a kind of permanent public record of their views, activities, and behavior. This public record can be thought of as an online reputation, which may be accessible to schools, employers, colleges, clubs, and others who may be researching an individual now or in the future. Cyberbullying can harm the online reputations of everyone involved—not just the person being bullied, but those doing the bullying or participating in it.[20]

Can anything be done to counteract the aforementioned negative effects to children not being given a voice at school? The answer to that question will be discussed in Section 3, Chapter 12.

* * *

CHAPTER 8

When Children Lack a Voice at Church

In Chapter 3 I looked at how false prophets, church cliques, church bullies, and individual factors can rob children of having a voice in churches. In this chapter I will explore possible consequences of children being unheard in churches. Bearing in mind that parental influence and the parents' reactions to children not being heard by church leaders plays a big role in the outcome. For example, if parents attend a church where false prophets are in leadership, the child may or may not have any say so as to whether that child continues to attend that particular church.

Often people "react to bullies in the congregation by leaving the church".[21] I know of one case where a young person in a church felt bullied by individuals critical of the behaviors of teenagers, such as attending ballgames and movies. As soon as this person was old enough, that person left the church to join one that gave young people a voice and where the leadership was encouraging of the younger people rather than critical.

Besides a person deciding to leave a church, what other possible outcomes of children not being heard by false prophets, church cliques, and church bullies exist? How do individual factors affect children that go unheard in church settings?

False Prophets Leave Unhealthy Legacies

False prophets teaching false doctrine can leave lifetime scars on young people. I have heard countless stories of individuals who grew up in legalistic churches that expressed little love and who were left with a sour taste in their mouth towards God and anything to do with any religion. Some of these people carry false guilt and anger for years until God intervenes to lead them to the truth and to bring healing to their wounds. Others never recover and die bitter against God and the world.

Churches sometimes try to protect false teachers, who might be better referred to as wolves in sheep's clothing (Matthew 7:15). In at least two cases I know about where ministers were molesting children in a specific congregation, the church leaders swept the abuse under the rug to protect the reputation of the church. These child molesters posing as ministers in the pulpit were only given a slap on the wrist, kicked out of the church, and not reported to the proper authorities. It angers me that these men were left out in the community to continue molesting children. No denomination is immune to such scandals though the Catholic Church seems to have been more in the news about this matter.

Church Cliques Exclude Others

Cliques within the church can be a huge detriment to all your ministry efforts, including spiritual growth, discipleship, community, and outreach. People can feel unloved, unnoticed, unimportant, and isolated.

A church with a strong culture of cliques and an "us vs. them" mentality will likely lose many members, simply because they never felt like they fit in or could find their place within the work and mission of the church. [22]

For students, according to YouthMinistry.com, "Cliques are the enemy of healthy community and ultimately the enemy of students hearing God's best for them. When students don't feel relationally comfortable, they are less likely to relate to God's truth." [23]

"Cliques are the enemy of healthy community and ultimately the enemy of students hearing God's best for them." —YouthMinistry.com

Church Bullies

I loved my middle school youth ministry. My high school youth group, not so much. In fact, I left after a year and switched to the youth group of a different church, even though I kept attending my old church on Sunday's. The reason? Bullying.

There were two boys who kept making degrading remarks about my weight—and the leaders did nothing. I complained, my parents complained, but nothing happened. So I stopped coming. One night, two of the elders of the church came for a visit with my parents and they wanted to know why I had stopped coming. They'd heard I was attending this other youth group and wanted to make sure my parents knew this church was 'liberal' (I grew up conservative Baptist and this church was a more liberal Baptist church). My dad got very upset with them and told them exactly why I had stopped coming. After that, the youth leaders made a half-hearted attempt to 'woo' me back, but I had completely lost my trust in them.[24]

The above account written by a victim of church bullies exemplifies so well what can happen when a child is not heard at church. Fortunately, the victim was resilient enough to not lose her faith. But not every case ends that well.

What are other possible outcomes? Just as students bullied at school suffer more depression and other emotional and psychological problems, it stands to reason that student members of a youth group who are bullied would also be at greater risk of such disorders. In the worst case scenario, a bullied youth group member may even choose to commit suicide.

Influence of Individual Factors

When a child is unheard at church, I believe that child's level of resiliency, amount of family support, health issues, and temperament or personality can either offset or exacerbate negative consequences that might result from the child not being heard.

Resiliency. In hindsight, I believe I had a high level of resiliency as a child due to my high intelligence and due to the positive influence and mentoring of my paternal grandmother. Thus, when I had no voice at church I was not affected in a negative way like other children who were not as resilient.

Family Support. The story told previously of the young girl bullied by two boys in her youth group is a perfect example of how one's family's support can make a negative situation more bearable. Unfortunately, not all children in churches have supportive parents to offset their pain of not being heard in a church setting.

Health Issues. Health issues, particularly mental and emotional problems, can exacerbate negative consequences of a child not being heard at church. For example, I think of a child that struggles with depression and/or low self-esteem. That child may have a stronger negative reaction than a child not struggling with depression or esteem issues. Additionally, I can even envision a case where a child might have a voice at church but due to depression or another mental disorder, it may only be a child's interpretation that he or she is not being heard and not, in fact, reality.

Child's temperament/personality. Temperament and personality also affect whether and how a child reacts to not having a voice at church. For example, an introverted child may not want attention and may not care whether he or she is seen or heard at church, while the outgoing child who craves attention might be more upset by not being heard by someone at church.

In closing, I would like to point out that I think the biggest factor in a child's reacting to whether he or she has a voice at church is whether that child has a personal relationship with God. I believe knowing and having a healthy, mature relationship with God can offset any negative factor in a child's life. For example, I know God's presence in my heart as a child enabled me to overcome a lot of disadvantages I had back then.

* * *

CHAPTER 9

When "The System" Fails

In Chapter 4, I discussed how child victims are often silenced by "the system". In particular, I shared how my own voice was silenced by the courts when I witnessed a horrendous crime at a young age. In Chapter 4 I also reported how the foster care system fails children today and has for decades. In this chapter I want to focus on the consequences of what happened when the courts made the case of which I was a witness go away. Then I will discuss what happens when the foster care system fails children and families today.

My Story Continues

"What you are describing is Complex PTSD. You need to read the book entitled *Complex PTSD* written by Pete Walker," H. Norman Wright, a grief and trauma specialist I met at the 2017 AACC World Conference, said after I shared with him bits and pieces of my story. I thought, *I'll have to get that book*, as I scribbled down the title and author's name on a piece of paper.

After reading *Complex PTSD: From Surviving to Thriving* (CreateSpace Independent Publishing, 2013), I had to agree with Dr. Wright's assessment. I had struggled with cPTSD since the day I witnessed the attempted rape and murder. Since I never received any form of treatment or counsel at the time of the trauma, the cPTSD only progressed until I received treatment for depression, anxiety, and codependency as an adult. What is cPTSD?

Walker (2013) defines this proposed psychological disorder Complex PTSD as "a more severe form of Post-traumatic stress disorder. It is delineated from this better known trauma syndrome by five of its most common and troublesome features: emotional flashbacks, toxic shame, self-abandonment, a vicious inner critic, and social anxiety." (p. 3) [25]

I have experienced all of the five symptoms mentioned by Walker some of which I struggle with today at times. For example, the process of writing this book is triggering emotional flashbacks that are causing me physical symptoms, such as nausea. My prayer is that writing this book will take me to deeper levels of healing as well as help other individuals with testimonies similar to mine.

Most of us are familiar with the "fight/flight" instinct responses that occur when a person is in danger. These are inborn healthy responses of the autonomic nervous system when an individual is faced with danger—either stand up and fight or flee in the opposite direction. Walker (2013) believes a more thorough and precise description of possible responses to danger are fight/flight/freeze/fawn. Walker reported that

> *Traumatized children often over-gravitate to one of these response patterns to survive, and as time passes these four modes become elaborated into entrenched defensive structures that are similar to narcissistic [fight], obsessive/compulsive [flight], dissociative [freeze] or codependent [fawn] defenses. (p. 13)*

I recall having experienced all four of the aforementioned reactions to danger at different points in time...

...the two symptoms I see most throughout my life are the internal critic and catastrophizing. I've always been my own worst critic, which reflects a perfectionistic nature. Catastrophizing is always thinking of the worst possible outcome. I

still have problems with this phenomenon, especially riding in the car with someone. A recent example occurred when my husband and I were riding down the road. A police officer had a man pulled over. When my husband failed to obey the traffic law to get in the far lane, I rebuked him, as I imagined us in the middle of a shoot-out.[26].

For more information about my story, I invite you to visit the blog at my husband's and my webpage, https://abcsministries. wordpress.com/. Articles I recommend are "Complex PTSD... No Easy Battle", "Sexual Abuse & Witnessing a Murder...It only happens in the movies. Wrong! It happened to me", and "What a Shock!—How God Prepared Me".

When Foster Care Fails

Foster care was intended to be a temporary solution for children who could not be safely left at home.[27] *It was seen as better than the orphanage and as a means "to create a nurturing family environment without infringing on the rights of the parents."*[28]

Children in foster care can be placed with a relative, with a licensed foster family, or at a residential facility. Based on research and my experience as a foster mother, the system has failed many children placed in foster care by not fulfilling the original purpose of the program. Many foster children have ended up staying in the system for years, often having lived at multiple locales, either group homes or with more than one foster family.

What grieves me the most is that many of these children are abused while in state custody. Why does this happen? It is my understanding that the motives for many foster parents doing so is for the money rather than out of a pure heart wanting to help children. Employees at group homes burn out, just as many case workers do. These employees, if they don't quit, can become abusive to the residents, whether intentional or not.

What happens to youths raised in our chaotic and dysfunctional foster care system? The outlook for most is grim, given their histories of broken relationships and unstable educational experiences. They are far more likely to become teen parents, be chronically unemployed, and spend their lives in poverty than other young people.

Moreover, recent studies have shown that young adults exiting the foster care system are prime targets for predators running sex-trafficking rings. In a study of youths held for prostitution in California, for example, most had come from foster care.[29]

Before closing, I want to point out that I do not believe that a child placed in foster care is destined to have a tragic ending. There are exceptions, as I have known of children taken by the state who were in time adopted by loving grandparents. The outcome of these children was more favorable than the typical outcomes discussed previously.

* * *

CHAPTER 10

Repercussions of Unheard Children in Society

In Chapter 5 I discussed social taboos, false beliefs that wreak havoc in children's lives, including

- "Family Secrets" are okay.
- Children are to be seen, and not heard.
- Fighting is a good way to resolve conflict.
- Sticks and stones may break my bones, but words can never hurt me.
- Other messages that fail to see children through God's eyes

Since it would have been difficult for a participant to assess whether negative consequences of not being heard as a child were caused by parents, teachers, pastors, or others, in the *Children without Voices* survey I asked general questions about the consequences of not being heard as a child. The results to the responses of these questions are found in tables in Appendix B.

Short-term consequences exist that one might experience as a child. Those that I asked about include:

- Anxiety (See Table 6)
- Depression (See Table 7)
- Suicidal ideation (See Table 8)
- Indifference (See Table 9)

In my own experience, I suffered long term consequences as an adult that I have no doubt stemmed from my having no voice as a child. These consequences were:

- Anxiety (See Table 10)
- Depression (See Table 11)
- Low self-esteem (See Table 12)
- Suicidal ideation (See Table 13)
- Trust issues (See Table 14)
- Relationship problems (See Table 15)

In addition to the specific issues listed previously, I also asked respondents whether there were other long-term effects of not feeling heard as a child that he or she experienced. See Table 16 for their responses. Many of the other reported long-term effects mimic those of someone with past sexual abuse. For this reason and because of the increasing amount of sexual abuse in society, which robs victims of their voices leaving devastating life-long scars, I will focus on the harm done to sexual abuse victims in the remainder of this chapter.

In an article entitled "Young Victims of Sex Abuse Go Unheard", *Washington Post* Reporter Robert O'Harrow, Jr. reported that

In an unpublished survey of 600 prosecutors' offices nationwide, the American Bar Association's Center on Children and the Law found that the main reason prosecutors rejected sexual abuse cases was problems with having a child witness. Nearly two-thirds said they sometimes or very often rejected cases because the victim was too young.[30]

This report reminds me of my case where I was told by the courts that I was too young to testify against an adult whom I had witnessed committing an attempted rape and murder.

On any given day one can go on the Internet to read about another child victim of sexual abuse. We read of young children sexually molested, of young girls forced into prostitution and sex trafficking, and other horrendous sex crimes. Other child victims of the sex industry that often go overlooked are the children of prostitutes.[31]

What are the consequences of all the sex related violations rampant in society that rob children's voices? According to Darkness to Light (d2l), sexual abuse impacts society economically, socially, and health wise.

Financial Costs to Society

The health and social impacts of child sexual abuse on a survivor last a lifetime and affect us all socially and financially. The average lifetime cost per victim of child abuse is $210,012[32], costing the U.S. billions annually.

These expenses are largely paid for by the public sector— the taxpayer.[33]

These expenses include:

- Medical costs
- Court costs
- Welfare costs for children
- Special education expenses
- Productivity losses

Social Repercussions of Sexual Abuse

Other than the burden of the financial costs of child sexual abuse, society also suffers in other ways when children are abused. These repercussions include a higher crime rate, more problems in schools, teenage pregnancy, and other problems related to sexual behavior. According to d2l, "Adult survivors are

> **Sexual abuse impacts society economically, socially, and health wise. —d2l**

also more likely to become involved in crime, both as a perpetrator and as a victim."[34]

Physical, Mental, & Emotional Damage to Survivors

As a former victim of early childhood sexual abuse and as a Christian counselor and life coach specializing in issues of abuse, I know full well about the physical, mental and emotional damage that results in survivors.

Physical problems. Personally, I have experienced a lot of stress-related physical problems that I have no doubt were linked either directly or indirectly to the abuse I experienced as a child. Among these health issues are GERD, TMD, nervous bladder, and high blood pressure. Other stress-related physical health concerns that sexual abuse survivors can experience include ulcers, intestinal problems, lower backaches, stiff neck, tight jaw, and chronic headaches.

Obesity also is common among sexual abuse victims. Though I was never obese growing up, I did carry more weight than my female peers at school. In hindsight, this was my attempt subconsciously to make myself unattractive to the opposite sex. For a more in depth discussion linking sexual abuse and disordered eating, please see Chapter 18 entitled "Linking Disordered Eating with Sexual Abuse" in the book *Food as an Idol: The Types, Causes, Consequences, Conquering, and Prevention of Disordered Eating* (ABC's Ministries, 2019).

Mental/emotional problems. The fallout from sexual abuse on one's mind and emotions can be devastating and often leaves lifelong scars. That fallout can include:

- False guilt and shame. Often victims of sexual abuse will carry guilt and shame blaming themselves for years for what happened. In reality, the perpetrator should carry all the burden of guilt and shame.
- Ambivalence. This is where the victim has conflicting feelings towards a situation. For example, this commonly occurs

in marriages where a spouse with past sexual abuse may struggle with conflicting feelings towards having sex with his or her mate.

- Suicide and depression. Depression, which can end in suicide, also occurs in sex abuse survivors. I remember suicidal ideation as being a common struggle for me during my recovery process.

- Sexual dysfunction. An example of sexual dysfunction would be when a survivor lacks any desire for sex as a result of the abuse.

- Unhealthy body image. Unhealthy body image, often linked to eating disorders and/or low self-esteem, also can occur in survivors of sexual abuse.

- A desire to self-injure. Some sexual abuse survivors cut themselves. I knew a woman who did this. She said the pain from cutting kept her from having to face the pain of the abuse.

- OCD response. In my own case, I remember having OCD symptoms as far back as high school. In high school, I was obsessed with having to make the grade. After I got out of school, the symptoms carried over into my housekeeping where I thought I had to have a spotless house. Not anymore!!!

- PTSD response. We hear a lot about PTSD in adults but it also can occur in children. The effects of sexual abuse on a child vary depending on the nature of the abuse, family support, and community support. Examples of PTSD symptoms that can occur in children include acting out, irrational fears, nervousness, and nightmares.

- Dissociative disorder responses. What is dissociation? In simplest terms, dissociation is the splitting off from reality. "There are five main ways in which the dissociation of psychological processes changes the way a person experiences living: depersonalization, derealization, amnesia, identity confusion, and identity alteration."[35]

Personally, though the effects of sexual abuse can be devastating, I believe God can redeem the damage enabling the survivor to live a healthy fulfilling life. I am living proof of that. Some have even referred to me as "a walking miracle".

* * *

SECTION THREE:

Solutions to Children Feeling Unheard

- For Parents
- For Educators
- In the Church
- Legal Issues
- For Society

CHAPTER 11

Parenting Practices That Work

One of the most important psychological factors in raising a family is giving children "voice." What is "voice"? It is the sense of agency that resides in all of us, that makes us confident that we will be heard, and that we will have impact on our environment. Exceptional parents grant a child a voice equal to theirs the day that child is born. And they respect that voice as much as they respect their own.[36]

How can parents give a child "voice"? Psychologist Richard Grossman, Ph.D. recommends three practices that give a child voice.[37] They are

- Consider anything a child says just as significant as anything the parent has to say.
- Remember parents can learn from their children just as children learn from parents.
- Parents should connect with a child through entering the child's world (e.g. play) rather than expecting the child to relate at an adult level.

Throughout the book *Listening to Children: Talking with Children about Difficult Issues* (Allyn & Bacon, 2002) Nancy Close stresses three key points to communicating with children effectively. They are:

- Always respect and be interested in what a child says.

- Always talk to a child on his or her level.
- Don't overwhelm a child asking too many questions or giving more information than necessary.

Listening is a key to having a healthy relationship with a child and to giving that child a sense of security. What are things parents can do to improve their listening skills? According to the website beingtheparent.com, to improve their listening skills parents should do the following:

- ***Practice active listening*** *and focus on what the child is trying to say without forming or mouthing any opinions.*
- ***Place yourself in your child's shoes****, imagine how you would have reacted in a given situation that your child is in.*
- ***Be present physically and mentally.*** *When you get your child to talk, be fully in the moment. The dishes can wait, so can your phone calls. Let your child know he has your undivided attention.*
- ***Notice your child's body language*** *and decode the non-verbal things your child is trying to say.*
- ***Show curiosity and have an open mind.*** *You should not be judgmental when it comes to listening to anyone.*[38]

Not only is listening to what the child has to say important but what we say and the manner in which what we say is said also is very important to having healthy communication with a child.

It is important to talk with a child in a manner that is not condescending and that communicates to the child, "I am listening and I am interested in what you have to tell me." Children readily pick out adults who talk with them and not at them and know which ones will listen to them.[39]

Even with the best of parenting skills in giving children voice, remember conflicts will occur between parents and children. What are some healthy conflict resolution skills that parents can use with children? The following is a list adapted from Michael and Amy Smalley's "ground rules for fair fighting:[40]"

- Be clear in defining the problem.
- Don't ignore the problem.
- Listen attentively repeating back what the child says.
- Stay in the here and now. Don't bring up past mistakes.
- Don't argue the details.
- Don't get into power struggles.
- Don't judge. Use "I" statements.
- Always be honest in what you share.
- Avoid discussions when angry. Cool off first.
- Break when necessary but don't just walk out. Agree to resume later.
- Avoid using the silent treatment.
- Always love unconditionally.
- Don't resort to sarcasm or violence to solve problems.
- Don't exaggerate the problem making mountains out of molehills.
- Confront privately when possible and appropriate.
- Don't involve unnecessary third parties.
- Compliment rather than discourage.
- Don't lecture. Be specific about offenses committed.
- Show love outwardly during conflicting discussions.
- Empathize with your child.
- Remember each child is unique. Don't compare your children to each other.
- Treat each child as an individual.
- Take responsibility when you've been wrong.
- Be clear about future expectations.

- Work together to come to a mutual agreement.
- Offer forgiveness when needed.
- Always be respectful when resolving a conflict.
- Solve disagreements promptly.

Now I would like to share a few additional tips from the respondents of the *Children without Voices* survey. The suggestions were in response to the question asking how we can prevent children from feeling like they have no voice in the home. Among the suggestions are:

- Have family meetings where children can share concerns about family matters.
- Have frequent conversations letting them know their part in the family and helping them to understand their value.
- Have family meals together.
- Have one on one time with each child.
- Both parents and children need to be taught how to have healthy boundaries.
- Give children responsibilities in the home. This makes room for interaction.
- Parents need to do the work on their own issues. Otherwise, one way or another it will affect their children and all relationships really. The most important one being that with themselves.
- Parents need to understand that children are created by God as an individual.

Before closing this chapter, I would like to share key Scriptures that I believe are very important for parents to know and follow:

"Train up a child in the way he should go, And when he is old he will not depart from it" (Proverbs 22:6).

"He who spares his rod hates his son, But he who loves him disciplines him promptly" (Proverbs 13:24).

"And you, fathers, do not provoke your children to wrath, but bring them up in the training and admonition of the Lord" (Ephesians 6:4).

"Fathers, do not provoke your children, lest they become discouraged" (Colossians 3:21).

Parents who practice the healthy communication and conflict resolution skills given in this chapter give their children a "voice". Based on my own personal experience, I believe only by giving children a voice can a parent gain the full trust and respect of their children.

In closing this chapter, I want to offer a final Word from the Lord to parents. Remember no child asked to be brought into this world. In compliance with Scripture, I ask parents to remember and treat each child as a gift from the Lord.

Behold, children *are* a heritage from the Lord, The fruit of the womb *is* a reward" (Psalm 127:3, NKJV).

* * *

CHAPTER 12

Sounding Unheard Voices at School

'Student voice' is the individual and collective perspective and actions of students within the context of learning and education. Not only can it change the education climate of a school effectively, it can also strengthen student achievement and foster workforce readiness. Every single student in every classroom has a voice that should be engaged in schools. Student voice allows students to share who they are, what they believe in, and why they believe what they do, with their peers, parents, teachers and their entire school.[41]

In Chapter 2 how unsupportive teachers and other school officials, how competition among students for the teacher's attention, and how bullying can rob students of voice at school were discussed, In Chapter 7 I looked at the consequences of students being unheard in the classroom due to the causes discussed in the earlier chapter. In this chapter I propose to offer solutions that enable all students to have a healthy voice at school.

Teachers Giving Voice to Students

In my generation my classmates and I grew up where the role of the teacher was orator, director, and sage, or expert. Today's classrooms have changed.

In an era of increased accountability and measured student outcomes, student voice represents a growing movement in education. Instead of a top down, teacher directed approach to learning, students play an active and equal role in planning, learning, and leading their classroom instruction as well as contributing to the development of school practices and policies. This significant philosophical shift requires all stakeholders to embrace the belief that there is something to learn from every individual regardless of age, culture, socioeconomic status, or other qualifying factors.[42]

What techniques can be used in the classroom by teachers to give students more voice? Teachers and other school officials should offer students more "choice, control, challenge, and opportunities for collaboration".[43] Doing so increases student morale and students' desire to engage, which both affect academic success in positive ways.

> Teachers and other school officials should offer students more "choice, control, challenge, and opportunities for collaboration". — St.John and Briel

Healthy Competition in the Classroom

Classroom competition is beneficial if it motivates students to apply themselves more in their classwork and if it helps students get enthusiastic about subject matter. For example, teachers can incorporate team competitions, such as science quiz games and spelling bees, to help students remember more as they view subject matter as more exciting.

Though not every student can win in classroom competition, when handled fairly with everyone treated respectfully, all students can see the experience as positive with no child's self-esteem damaged. In fact, "small disappointments help children become more resilient, according to child psychologist Tamar Chansky in her book *Freeing Your Child from Negative Thinking.*"[44]

How to Handle Bullying at School

The approach to bullying in schools is two-fold. First, as I believe the old adage, "Prevention is always the best medicine," I want to look at how to PREVENT bullying first. Then I will discuss when preventive measures fail, how to STOP bullying.

PREVENT bullying. "All 50 U.S. states require schools to have a bullying prevention policy."[45] With the strong link between bullying and the climate or environment at school, according to the APA, as cited in Chapter 7, it stands to reason that creating a positive school climate will minimize the amount of bullying in a school.

What are the components of a positive healthy school climate? The components vary and can include rules related to relationship, power, and the media. "*Social norm engineering* is a conscious process that builds a positive culture among student peers and school adults that becomes self-reinforcing. Like a healthy immune system, a positive school climate promotes optimal health and reduces the chances of dysfunction or disease."[46]

To create a positive school environment, the school leaders need to be healthy. They need to be positive role models themselves modeling integrity and respect for everyone. School leaders also need to be educated about and equipped to confront bullying. It's important that teachers recognize and respond to "gateway behaviors"[47]. These are small actions of a child, such as calling names, ignoring, and laughing at others, that may indicate bullying is about to happen.

Another key to preventing school bullying is to teach students "social and emotional learning (SEL)"[48]. SEL consists of teaching students about self and social awareness, about how to control self and relationships with others, and about how to make healthy responsible decisions. Students need to be taught how to empathize with others, how to work with others in groups, and they need to be offered bully simulations to teach them what to do if they are a victim or witness to bullying. Benefits to SEL include:

- Healthier emotional wellbeing in students
- Improved self-regulation in students

- Kinder, more thoughtful students
- Less anxiety, stress, and depression in students
- Less disruptive behaviors, including bullying
- Greater academic success, ingenuity, and leadership in students

STOP bullying. Despite all preventive measures, bullying may still occur at schools, especially when there are students who have bullying modeled at home or in other environments outside school. In such cases, what can be done to stop the bullying at school? The Crisis Prevention Institute (CPI) offers ten suggestions.[49] They are:

- Clearly define bullying. The CPI distinguishes between bullying and teasing. Bullying is where one student has some sort of power over another student, such as a larger stature.
- Never label a child "bully" or "victim". Target the behavior as being wrong instead.
- Establish clear and age-appropriate student guidelines regarding bullying and require adults at school to model and enforce the guidelines.
- Reinforce positive behavior. For example, compliment a child for doing something nice for another student.
- Communicate with students openly and honestly, for example, in classroom meetings.
- Get parents involved.
- Teachers and other adults at school should look for warning signs that a child is being bullied, such as unexplainable injuries or a drop in grades. They also should know the signs that a student is bullying others (e.g.: frequent fighting or trips to the principal's office).
- When bullying happens, deal with the situation immediately by clearing the scene of any bystanders and then dealing with the child doing the bullying and the one being

bullied. Interview witnesses to get the full picture of what is happening.

- Monitor locations where bullying occurs frequently, such as in hallways and bathrooms, on playgrounds, and on buses when adults are not around.
- All school officials should be aware of all state, local, and district laws about bullying.

Before closing this chapter, I would like to offer additional insight from participants of the *Children without Voices* survey regarding how to prevent children from feeling unheard at school and among their peers. Among the responses of suggestions to prevent children from feeling unheard at school are:

- Teach children resilience and not to take others' behaviors and attitudes personally.
- Parents need to teach children how to speak up and build their confidence to do so. If we teach them their true value at home, they will expect that value from others.
- Provide more one on one communication; smaller student to teacher ratio.
- Better teacher training
- Have more support workers.
- Offer more mental health services at school.
- Teachers should acknowledge each student in their classes daily.
- Bring God back into the schools!

To prevent children from feeling unheard among their peers, the survey participants recommended the following:

- Teach students to make good choices when making friends.
- Offer discussion groups in class where each child's opinion is heard.

- Teach students better manners, tolerance, and that no one is better than the other.
- Offer students courses on healthy communication.

In summary, the goal of every school administrator should be to make sure every child in school has a voice. When school administrators and teachers model respect, encourage healthy competition, and take the recommended steps to minimize bullying, I believe that school is headed in the right direction where every child on that campus will feel heard and understood.

* * *

CHAPTER 13

Giving Voice to Children in the Church

In Chapter 3 I pointed out how false prophets, church cliques, church bullies, and individual factors can rob children of having a voice in churches. In Chapter 8 I discussed the possible consequences of children being unheard in churches. In this chapter I offer suggestions to remedy the problem of children not being heard by the church. I also will discuss what church bodies can do to help prevent children from feeling unheard in society, based on suggestions from the *Children without Voices* respondents.

Silence the Voices of False Prophets

> "'Beware of false prophets, who come to you in sheep's clothing, but inwardly they are ravenous wolves" (Matthew 7:15, NKJV).

False prophets are commonplace in the church carrying false teachings. Examples include proponents of the "name it and claim it" and the prosperity doctrines. First, I want to point out that I believe the primary responsibility of protecting children from false teachers falls on the parents. With that said, what do parents do when these false teachers come on the television or radio airwaves? Personally, I would change the channel or turn off the television or radio. Why? Because we are told in Scripture to

> "23 Keep your heart with all diligence,
> For out of it *spring* the issues of life.

> [24] Put away from you a deceitful mouth,
> And put perverse lips far from you"
> (Proverbs 4:23-24, NKJV).

Like King Solomon in Proverbs, the Apostle Paul also recommends distancing oneself from false prophets:

> "[17] Now I urge you, brethren, note those who cause divisions and offenses, contrary to the doctrine which you learned, and avoid them. [18] For those who are such do not serve our Lord Jesus Christ, but their own belly, and by smooth words and flattering speech deceive the hearts of the simple" (Romans 16:17-18).

Turning off the television or radio at home or in the car when you hear false teaching is easy enough but what should parents do if these teachers are members of their home church, perhaps even the pastor? Personally, if a false teaching comes from the pulpit and is the predominant belief in a church one is attending, I recommend the family find another church that teaches sound biblical doctrine.

In cases where a false teaching comes from an individual member of a congregation, how should this situation be handled? As advocated by Paul in Titus 1, I recommend making the pastor and elders of the church aware of the situation to confront. When church elders are grounded in biblically sound doctrine, they will be able to recognize, rebuke, and resist false teaching.[50]

Combat Church Cliques through Unity

> "Behold, how good and how pleasant it is For brethren
> to dwell together in unity!" (Psalm 133:1, NKJV).

Since cliques divide, then the obvious solution to eliminating cliques in a church, whether in the youth group or the congregation as a whole is to promote unity. How should Christians respond to cliques being in their church?

The first response must always be prayer. We need to lift up these individuals in prayer, and seek God's will to be done in the situation. Praise God for his sovereignty because as we are told in Romans 8 He works all things for good for those who love him. Many times these cliques will be lead [sic] by one strong alpha-type individual; pray for that person particularly, that God would open his or her eyes to submit to His holy Word.

Further response to a church clique must conform to the instructions given to us in the Word of God. According to Matthew 18:15 we first go to our sinning brother or sister and demonstrate their fault to them. This should be done in a spirit of humbleness and with love.[51]

Beyond dealing with individual clique leaders and members, what more can be done to dissolve cliques in churches? Church leaders need to develop a vision of unity and inclusion for everyone who attends a church. This can be accomplished by having open communication lines where everyone has the opportunity to stay abreast of and participate in church activities. No one should go unnoticed or feel left out. One way of including everyone is to incorporate ice-breaker games in Sunday school classes and other groups that encourage random interaction.

Church leaders need to develop a vision of unity and inclusion for everyone who attends a church.

Respond to Church Bullies with Love

"[36] "Teacher, which is the great commandment in the law?" [37] Jesus said to him, "'You shall love the Lord your God with all your heart, with all your soul, and with all your mind.' [38] This is the first and great commandment. [39] And the second is like it: 'You shall love your neighbor as yourself'" (Matthew 22:36-39, NKJV).

If one finds him or herself being the victim of a church bully, what should the response be?

First, we should never try and get back at a bully or seek revenge (Rom. 12:17). As Christians, we know that this world is not perfect, but we are not the judge of the earth. God is the one who can judge the world in righteousness and repay everyone for the evil that they've done (Rom. 12:19). Instead, respond to your bully with kindness and love.[52]

What can church leaders do to prevent bullying among children where both the one bullying and the target of the bully will have a voice? First, I recommend that an environment of mutual respect be established in all Sunday school classes and other groups. Children should know that unkind and rude remarks or behavior will not be tolerated. Additionally, adults at church should be encouraged to be positive role models that reflect love and respect for everyone.

Treasure Individual Differences

"My brethren, do not hold the faith of our Lord Jesus Christ, the Lord of glory, with partiality" (James 2:1).

God doesn't play favorites when it comes to giving individual children a voice in churches. Nor should church members show favoritism to any child based on that child's level of resiliency, family support, health situation, or personality.

What more can churches do to help prevent children from feeling unheard in society? The *Children without Voices* participants offered these suggestions:

- Build stronger children's and youth ministries.
- Offer more programs in the church that meet the needs of children.
- Build stronger alliances with the parents. Teach parents how to be godly parents.

- Provide more opportunities for children to have their voices heard (e.g.: children's choir)
- Be a safe place for children to talk. Take the time to stop and listen.

Personally, the two greatest things I believe churches can do to give children a voice in the world is to teach them how loved and valued they are by God and to teach them the value of prayer.

* * *

CHAPTER 14

Hope for "The System"

In Chapter 4 and Chapter 9 I looked at how "the system", referring to social services, foster care, and legal entities, robs children of their voices and the consequences of them doing so. In this chapter I will be gleaning material from the prevention section of the book I wrote *We Survived Sexual Abuse! You Can Too!* (ABC's Ministries, 2016). I also will be drawing suggestions from the *Children without Voices* survey responses.

Key suggestions I made regarding the role of government and legislatures in preventing sexual abuse also are applicable to giving children a voice with the system and in society. These suggestions include:

- I believe "legislatures should require schools to offer to all students courses in character development in kindergarten through high school".[53] Why do I believe this? As I reported in *We Survived Sexual Abuse! You Can Too!*

"More and more educators are coming to realize that although the separation of church and state in America is part of our political heritage, our students must be educated to have common values of honesty, love, respect, and respon-sibility in their lives" (Allen & Coy, 2004, p. 355). Allen and Coy reported that only through teaching mutual respect and other positive character traits might an answer to reducing violence be found. Furthermore, Walsh (1998), as cited by

Allen and Coy, links character development, and spirituality to having resilience discussed previously.[54]

- Legislatures should "adopt a national 'bathroom bill' to protect women and children".[55] I firmly believe that legislation should be passed and enforced that requires individuals to use public restrooms and dressing rooms of the sex given on one's birth certificate. Why?

This keeps the safety of children a number one priority. Otherwise, the door is wide open for pedophiles and other sex offenders to dress in women's attire just to be able to enter a woman's restroom seeking potential victims. One such case has already occurred in a Target store in Texas. For the rare cases of Klinefelter's and other genetic or other biological anomalies, Orgeron suggests that a separate Family bathroom be available for such individuals to use.[56]

In the *Children without Voices* survey I asked the participants to give me one suggestion as to how our government can help children from feeling unheard in society. A few of the responses were quite negative which surprised me. These negative remarks included the following:

- Government officials have become an embarrassment.
- Government is the problem. We should be looking to God for help and NOT the government. [I do agree with the second part of this comment.]
- The government might need to stay out of this???
- The government should get out of schools.

A couple of the comments referred to elected government officials about how American citizens need to elect officials who really care about and will advocate for children and about how elected officials need to set the example that they want to see in their constituents. Other participants called for legislators to create better laws that need to be enforced, such as:

- Laws that protect children and punish perpetrators of children
- Laws that create accountability with educators and parents

Other participants suggested programs designed to help parents of children, including mandatory parenting classes and programs

"...American citizens need to elect officials who really care about and will advocate for children..."

that help families who live in poverty. A couple of participants recommended the government sponsor more children focused programs in schools and in the community, such as Boys' and Girls' Clubs, etc.

A number of the *Children without Voices* participants addressed the attitudes of our government towards children with the following comments:

- Be open to children.
- Be more mindful about children and their feelings. Just because they are small and do not know how to properly express themselves does not mean they have nothing to say.

One participant suggested letting children write letters to our government officials about issues they feel strongly about and having those leaders respond to the children positively.

Five final miscellaneous remarks regarding how the government can help give children a voice have to do with the following:

- Educating the public on sexual abuse effects and quit supporting people who support pedophiles
- Advocating for insurance companies to better cover mental health.

- The foster care system must treat every child as traumatized and offer services accordingly.

- Agencies that monitor or control child welfare and placement are old, broken and need to be changed to a system that puts the real, true focus on the children.

- Stop offering free services but charge in other ways. My children didn't go to private schools because I could not afford to. But the schools asked for so much money and donations it almost cost the same as tuition. There is no such thing as no child left behind. This is coming from a single mother with a child support order that is not being enforced because I have two jobs and not in the system. If I did not have two jobs I could not afford to send my son to public school as well as private.

Before I close this chapter I have two more concerns on my heart. First, I would be amiss to not advocate for another population of unheard children, aborted babies. Legislation needs to be passed and enforced that will protect these innocent lives who have never had a voice. I believe those who perform abortions and their accomplices should be prosecuted to the fullest for murder because that is what abortion is, murder. Agencies that support abortion, such as Planned Parenthood, should be forced to shut down or change their policies to no longer condone abortion.

My second concern involves how we have allowed God to be taken out of our schools. I believe legislatures need to reverse policies that removed prayer from schools and that prohibit educators from sharing their faith with students. I know had I not had Christian teachers who shared biblical truths with me at times I would not have coped as well as I did when circumstances were stressful at home. Additionally, I believe that America was founded on biblical principles and that today's legislators need to return to the faith of our Founding Fathers.

* * *

CHAPTER 15

Overcoming Societal Taboos: A Call for Revival and Spiritual Awakening

"If My people who are called by My name will humble themselves, and pray and seek My face, and turn from their wicked ways, then I will hear from heaven, and will forgive their sin and heal their land" (2 Chronicles 7:14, NKJV).

In this chapter first I will discuss based on research what can be done to overcome the societal taboos and the harm that these taboos create in children by robbing them of their voices. Then I will discuss unique suggestions not already reported that were made by the *Children without Voices* survey participants when I asked them how we can help prevent children from feeling unheard in society. I will conclude the chapter and book by discussing what I believe to be the ultimate solution to giving children back their voices in America.

In reviewing the literature, one recommendation that I found which I believe offers a lot of hope and the opportunity for healing from children's voices being silenced in the past is suggested by Sam Frankel in his book, *Giving Children a Voice* (Jessica Kingsley Publishers, 2018). Frankel proposes developing "a 'culture of advocacy' within your organization, home or indeed any setting that you share with children".[57] What does Frankel mean in suggesting a culture of advocacy for children?

A culture of advocacy is reflected in a setting in which:

• *Children's voices are acknowledged and valued*

- *Opportunities are created to make sure that children's voices are heard.*

Advocacy, in this context, is driven by the value that children's voices can bring to each and every setting that they experience, whether that is a home or school, a restaurant or courtroom, a playground or shopping mall.[58]

Although Frankel's book focuses on how having a culture of advocacy has been implemented in schools in England, I believe this approach also needs to be promoted in America. Obviously, one of the *Children without Voices* survey respondents would agree with Frankel, as the following comment was made.

Only when new laws allow and we have good child advocates especially for the abused child. Education in parenting with good follow up care inside the home as well as outside the home. With "at risk children" having double dose follow up. Society can only make things better by education, encouragement and empowering the new parents. It takes a village.... or a church.
Especially for those single parents.

What might it look like if a culture of advocacy were implemented in America? First, let's look at what it means to be an advocate. According to dictionary.com, an advocate is "a person who speaks or writes in support or defense of a person, cause, etc. (usually followed by of) an advocate of peace".

If more Americans became advocates for children I can envision our country having a lot less problems in society such as those discussed in Section 2 of this book. Can you imagine how much less child abuse, bullying, mental and emotional problems, and crime there could be if more citizens would advocate for children? What would this look like? I suggest the following changes would occur:

- No more covering up of child abuse whether at home, at school, at church, or in any other setting

- More educational resources available to children and adults that teach healthy communication and conflict resolution skills
- More and better interventions to STOP bullying, whether at school, church, or through the Internet

Can you imagine how much less child abuse, bullying, mental and emotional problems, and crime there could be if more citizens would advocate for children?

What more can we do to give children a voice in society? Here are a few unique suggestions made by the *Children without Voices* participants:

- Encourage children to get involved in community activities, especially volunteering.
- Challenge media viewpoints, such as children are not smart enough or experienced enough to have thoughts and feelings.
- Parents should be given the tools to screen social media sites to protect children from perpetrators.
- Teach children how to use the phone to call people. Teach them how to check out at the grocery store or other stores and how to interact with the checkout people. Sign them up for a bank account and have them deposit a few dollars a month inside with the teller. Let them order their own food at the restaurant. Take them to free museums and talk with a tour guide and encourage questions.
- Help seek out that which each child displays an interest in, such as a sport, such as building a spiritual connection. We have to show up and display that they are worthy to be seen and heard.
- If we can teach our children to honor everyone's life and value as a person, they will grow up, hopefully, to teach their children the same and that should change a generation.

Another comment that I want to share made by a *Children without Voices* survey participant stated, "We need to get back to the principles of God." I saved this quote because I believe it contains the thrust of what it will take to heal our land from the harm done by children not having a voice in the past. Americans, we need to fall on our faces to repent of the atrocities committed against our children, atrocities, such as child abuse and neglect, abortion, and others.

Healing and restoration can only come through the power of Jesus Christ. Maybe someone out there thinks, *I wasn't listened to as a child so I don't have a good example to follow.* I encourage them to follow the example of Jesus Christ. For a biblical path to healing, the path I followed, see Appendix C. For those who don't believe me, consider the testimony of one of the *Children without Voices* survey participants. When I asked about additional long term effects of not being heard as a child, this person wrote, "I had many, but I feel many are resolved due to making Jesus the Lord of my life. It is His opinion that counts, not an abuser."

While the focus of *Why Didn't They Hear Us?* has been on the causes, consequences, and solutions to children feeling unheard, I believe God's ultimate purpose in having me write this book is to call America to revival and spiritual awakening. Some may wonder what the difference between the two concepts is.

Simply stated, the biggest difference is in the population that each concept applies to: Revival applies to the church, professing believers in Jesus Christ; spiritual awakening applies to the lost, those persons who do not know Jesus as Lord and Savior[59].

Are you in need of revival? Then I encourage you to repent and turn back to God. For those who have never accepted Jesus Christ as Lord and Savior, I invite you to follow the steps to salvation given in Appendix D.

* * *

APPENDIXES

APPENDIX A

Children without Voices Survey

1. Sex:
   Answer Choices:

   - Male
   - Female
   - Prefer not to answer

2. Age:
   Answer Choices:

   - 18-24
   - 25-34
   - 35-44
   - 45-54
   - 55-64
   - 65+

3. Childhood Background
   Answer Choices:

   - Raised in a traditional family (Mom & Dad with siblings)
   - Raised in a traditional family (Mom & Dad, no siblings)
   - Single-Parent Family

- Blended Family (e.g.: Mom, Dad, his children, her children, and their children)
- Adopted Child
- Foster Child

4. Did you feel listened to by your parents or other primary caregiver in your childhood?
   Answer Choices: Always, Usually, Sometimes, Rarely, Never

5. Did you feel listened to by your teachers?
   Answer Choices: Always, Usually, Sometimes, Rarely, Never

6. Did you feel listened to by your peers/classmates?
   Answer Choices: Always, Usually, Sometimes, Rarely, Never

7. As a child, did you feel listened to in society (church, government, etc.), in general?
   Answer Choices: Always, Usually, Sometimes, Rarely, Never

8. Did you feel listened to by others? Please specify who below and how much they listened to you on a scale of 1to 5 with 1 being always and 5 being never.
   Fill in the Blank Answer

9. Regarding why you felt unheard by your parents or other primary caregiver, do you think parental/caregiver selfishness was the cause?
   Answer Choices: Always, Usually, Sometimes, Rarely, Never

10. Regarding why you felt unheard by your parents or other primary caregiver, do you think parental/caregiver ignorance was the cause?
    Answer Choices: Always, Usually, Sometimes, Rarely, Never

11. Regarding why you felt unheard by your parents or other primary caregiver, do you think parental/caregiver distractions, such as poor health or job responsibilities, were the cause?
Answer Choices: Always, Usually, Sometimes, Rarely, Never

12. Regarding why you felt unheard by your parents or other primary caregiver, do you think your own low self-esteem was the cause?
Answer Choices: Always, Usually, Sometimes, Rarely, Never

13. Regarding why you felt unheard by your parents or other primary caregiver, do you think sibling rivalry or jealousy was a cause?
Answer Choices: Always, Usually, Sometimes, Rarely, Never

14. Can you think of other factors that might have contributed to why you felt unheard by your parents or other primary caregiver as a child?
Answer Choices: Always, Usually, Sometimes, Rarely, Never

15. Did not feeling heard as a child make you feel anxious?
Answer Choices: Always, Usually, Sometimes, Rarely, Never

16. Did not feeling heard as a child make you feel depressed?
Answer Choices: Always, Usually, Sometimes, Rarely, Never

17. Did not feeling heard as a child make you feel suicidal?
Answer Choices: Always, Usually, Sometimes, Rarely, Never

18. Did not feeling heard as a child make you feel indifferent?
Answer Choices: Always, Usually, Sometimes, Rarely, Never

19. As an adult, have you experienced anxiety as a result of not being heard as a child?
Answer Choices: Always, Usually, Sometimes, Rarely, Never

20. As an adult, have you experienced depression as a result of not being heard as a child?

Answer Choices: Always, Usually, Sometimes, Rarely, Never

21. As an adult, have you experienced low self-esteem as a result of not being heard as a child?
Answer Choices: Always, Usually, Sometimes, Rarely, Never

22. As an adult, have you experienced suicidal thoughts as a result of not being heard as a child?
Answer Choices: Always, Usually, Sometimes, Rarely, Never

23. As an adult, have you experienced trust issues as a result of not being heard as a child?
Answer Choices: Always, Usually, Sometimes, Rarely, Never

24. As an adult, have you experienced relationship problems as a result of not being heard as a child?
Answer Choices: Always, Usually, Sometimes, Rarely, Never

25. Are there other long-term effects of not feeling heard as a child that you have experienced? Please specify.
Fill in the Blank Answer

26. Please offer one suggestion as to how we can prevent children from feeling like they have no voice in the home.
Fill in the Blank Answer

27. Please offer one suggestion as to how we can prevent children from feeling unheard at school.
Fill in the Blank Answer

28. Please offer one suggestion as to how we can help prevent children from feeling unheard among their peers?
Fill in the Blank Answer

29. Please offer one suggestion as to how we can help children from feeling unheard in society.

Fill in the Blank Answer

30. Please offer one suggestion as to how churches can help prevent children from feeling unheard in society.
Fill in the Blank Answer

31. Please offer one suggestion as to how our government can help prevent children from feeling unheard in society.
Fill in the Blank Answer

32. If you are a parent, do you think your children feel listened to by you?
Answer Choices: Always, Usually, Sometimes, Rarely, Never

33. If you are a parent, how much do you think you listen to your child?
Answer Choices:
A great deal, A lot, A moderate amount, A little, None at all

34. What are ways parents can listen to their children better?
Fill in the Blank Answer

35. Do you have any other comments, questions, or concerns regarding children without voices?
Fill in the Blank Answer

* * *

APPENDIX B

Consequences of Children Being Unheard Survey Results

TABLE 6: Did not feeling heard as a child make you feel anxious?

Answer Choices	Responses	Percentage
Always	2	4.26
Usually	14	29.79
Sometimes	17	36.17
Rarely	7	14.89
Never	7	14.89
TOTAL	47	

TABLE 7: Did not feeling heard as a child make you feel depressed?

Answer Choices	Responses	Percentage
Always	7	14.89
Usually	11	23.40
Sometimes	12	25.53
Rarely	10	21.28
Never	7	14.89
TOTAL	47	

TABLE 8: Did not feeling heard as a child make you feel suicidal?

Answer Choices	Responses	Percentage
Always	1	2.13
Usually	2	4.26

Sometimes	14	29.79
Rarely	10	21.28
Never	20	42.55
TOTAL	47	

TABLE 9: Did not feeling heard as a child make you feel indifferent?

Answer Choices	Responses	Percentage
Always	5	10.64
Usually	8	17.02
Sometimes	14	29.79
Rarely	10	21.28
Never	10	21.28
TOTAL	47	

TABLE 10: As an adult, have you experienced anxiety as a result of not being heard as a child?

Answer Choices	Responses	Percentage
Always	2	4.26
Usually	11	23.40
Sometimes	18	38.30
Rarely	5	10.64
Never	11	23.40
TOTAL	47	

TABLE 11: As an adult, have you experienced depression as a result of not being heard as a child?

Answer Choices	Responses	Percentage
Always	5	10.64
Usually	7	14.89
Sometimes	16	34.04
Rarely	4	8.51
Never	15	31.91
TOTAL	47	

TABLE 12: As an adult, have you experienced low self-esteem as a result of not being heard as a child?

Answer Choices	Responses	Percentage
Always	11	23.91
Usually	11	23.91
Sometimes	9	19.57
Rarely	6	13.04
Never	9	19.57
TOTAL	46	

TABLE 13: As an adult, have you experienced suicidal thoughts as a result of not being heard as a child?

Answer Choices	Responses	Percentage
Always	1	2.17
Usually	2	4.35
Sometimes	12	26.09
Rarely	10	21.74
Never	21	45.65
TOTAL	46	

TABLE 14: As an adult, have you experienced trust issues as a result of not being heard as a child?

Answer Choices	Responses	Percentage
Always	15	31.91
Usually	10	21.28
Sometimes	7	14.89
Rarely	6	12.77
Never	9	19.15
TOTAL	47	

TABLE 15: As an adult, have you experienced relationship problems as a result of not being heard as a child?

Answer Choices	Responses	Percentage
Always	9	19.15
Usually	14	29.79
Sometimes	12	25.53
Rarely	3	6.38
Never	9	19.15
TOTAL	47	

TABLE 16: Are there other long-term effects of not feeling heard as a child that you have experienced? Please specify.

(***Responses are in the original wording of the respondents as much as possible.***)

I had many, but I feel many are resolved due to making Jesus the Lord of my life. It is His opinion that counts, not an abuser.
Very sensitive to not being considered
In many ways not feeling heard as a child strengthened my resolve to get on. It was an "I'll show you" attitude.
I was heard once I chose to tell. Relationships with anybody are a challenge due to over analyzing everything.
Anxiety, depression, uselessness, loneliness, unimportant

I don't feel connected to my parents now.
I also tried extra hard to make sure I didn't make my children feel that way.
It took me years to realize that who I believed I was, wasn't who I was. And I started to work on my self-esteem and social anxiety and am now helping other people through their problems. But if I hadn't I would properly (*sic,* probably) still suffer.

I never wanted kids. Having any other close friends was not easy for me.

Struggling to be able to speak up and be heard
Not being clear about boundaries when saying yes or no

I am afraid to voice my opinion because I might get into trouble.

It's complicated. I was sexually abused by an older brother, and my parents knew about the earlier incidents. Protecting the family was the priority so everything stemmed from that.

I'm now a poet.

I'm not important to the people who should care about me the most.

Having good, strong, relationships with friends is hard because I didn't always feel loved by parents, which left me sometimes thinking I am unlovable, and I pull away.

Eating disorders and addictions

Parenting has been challenging and has helped me to grow.

Low self-esteem, weight gain, poor body image, codependent, perfectionist

I ended up with an abusive husband reliving the cycles.

I felt like the Girl Nobody Wanted; also I had to find ways to protect myself from wuther (sic, further) harm. Questioning Who Am I?

Inability to bond with others

I think it has resulted in me being hyper involved in the lives of my own children.

Alcoholic, self-harm, drug issues

I have trouble knowing how to deal with my own past. I have trouble forgiving others. I have trouble knowing that I am accepted.
Do not trust anyone, no relationship with my parents
I wish that My parents had let me be more open. I have a good life; but, it could have been better.
Not feeling worthy
Not knowing myself

* * *

APPENDIX C

A Biblical Path From Discovery to Recovery

1. Face the problem. Identify the symptoms. I Corinthians 11:28.

2. Recount the incident. Verbalize the details.	Nehemiah 2	3. Experience past and present emotions.

4. Place the responsibility on the offender. Joshua 7.

5. Trace problem behaviors to their origin. Replace them with healthy behaviors.

6. Observe others. Educate yourself.

7. Confront the aggressor. Matthew 18:15.

8. Forgive. Colossians 3:13.

9. Rebuild self-esteem and relationships. Nehemiah 4:17.

10. Reach out to others. II Corinthians 1:3-4.

Figure 6 THE CROSS (Owens, 2001, Figure 2): A Biblical path to healing, based on Don and Jan Frank's 10 step "Critical Path Method for Emotional Recovery" from *When Victims Marry: Building a Stronger Marriage by Breaking Destructive Cycles (Here's Life, 1990)*, pp. 106-116.[60]

APPENDIX D

The **ABC's** of Salvation

Admit that you are a sinner.

A "^{23} for all have sinned and fall short of the glory of God,"

Romans 3:23

"^{23} For the wages of sin *is* death, but the gift of God *is* eternal life in Christ Jesus our Lord."

Romans 6:23

Believe in the Lord, Jesus Christ.

B "^{16} For God so loved the world that He gave His only begotten Son, that whoever believes in Him should not perish but have everlasting life."

John 3:16

Choose to confess and accept the gift of salvation.

C "^{10} For with the heart one believes unto righteousness, and with the mouth confession is made unto salvation."

Romans 10:10

Figure : The ABC's of Salvation[61]

GLOSSARY

ambivalence—This is where a victim has conflicting feelings towards a situation. For example, this commonly occurs in marriages where a spouse with past sexual abuse may struggle with conflicting feelings towards having sex with his or her mate.

authoritarian parents—Could be compared to a dictator. They have rigid standards offering children no say so in what happens in the family.

authoritative parents—The most advantageous of the parenting styles to children. They offer children loving limits, healthy communication, and realistic expectations.

catastrophizing—Always thinking of the worst possible outcome in a situation.

cognitive dissonance—This is where a person needs to adjust their behaviors to agree with their knowledge (e.g.: a person knows smoking is harmful to one's health but continues to smoke anyway).

dissociation—In simplest, terms, dissociation is the splitting off from reality (e.g.: amnesia, depersonalization, identity confusion).

Klinefelter syndrome—"A genetic condition that results when a boy is born with an extra copy of the X chromosome. Klinefelter syndrome is a genetic condition affecting males, and it often isn't diagnosed until adulthood."[62]

learned helplessness—Due to trauma or repeated negative exposure to derogatory remarks from others about self, a child grows up to be irresponsible after learning helplessness from past experience.

neglectful parents—Fail to get involved in the lives of their children and communicate very little with them.

parens patriae—Refers to when the government steps in to protect a child unable to protect him or herself.

parenting—In simplest terms refers to child rearing. A broader definition would be the processes, guidance, etc. offered to children from birth to adulthood that promotes their development, including physical, emotional, intellectual, psychological, social, and spiritual.

permissive parents—Typically indulge their children and offer little if any structure to allow each child to do whatever he or she wants.

resilience—The concept that is used to describe the flexibility that allows certain children to cope with and manage major difficulties and disadvantages in life, and even to thrive in the face of what appear to be overwhelming odds.

self-fulfilling prophecy—According to the APA Dictionary of Psychology, this is "a belief or expectation that helps to bring about its own fulfillment, as, for example, when a person expects nervousness to impair his or her performance in a job interview or when a teacher's preconceptions about a student's ability influence the child's achievement for better or worse."[63]

social norm engineering—A conscious process that builds a positive culture among student peers and school adults that becomes self-reinforcing.

* * *

NOTES

1. Beckelman, *Cry of Beaten Child,* 1-2.

2. Beckelman, 5-6.

3. Rainer, *Fourteen Symptoms of Toxic.*

4. Rainer, ¶2.

5. Gambill, *When Bullying Comes,* ¶5.

6. Orgeron, *We Survived,* 45.

7. Beckelman, *Cry of Beaten Child*; Burton, *System is Failing*; Robinson, *Remedying Our Foster*; Sankaran, *In Court, Children.*

8. Robinson, *Remedying Our Foster,* 395.

9. Beckelman, *Cry of Beaten Child,* ¶18.

10. Sankaran, *In Court, Children,* ¶4.

11. Beckelman, *Cry of Beaten Child,* ¶4.

12. Writing Explained, Children Seen Not Heard Meaning, ¶1-2.

13. St.John, *Why Raising Children,* 3.

14. Martin, *Sticks and Stones,* What's the origin…, ¶1.

15. Orgeron, *We Survived,* 64.

16. Whealin and Barnett, *Child Sexual Abuse,* What are the Effects of Childhood Sexual Abuse?, ¶5.

17. Pychyl, *Personality Homework Behavior,* ¶2.

18. American Psychological Association, *Bullying School Climate*; *Bullying in Schools*; Dake et.al., *Nature Extent of* ; Olweus, *Annotation: Bullying…* ; Tuten, *Hurt Kids Hurt*; U.S. Department of Health and Human Services, *What is Cyberbullying.*

19. Tuten, *Hurt Kids Hurt,* ¶5.

20. U.S. Department of Health and Human Services, *What is Cyberbullying*, Special Concerns, ¶1.

21. Alsgaard, *Bullying happens in church*, Deal with the situation, ¶3.

22. McDonald, *Fighting the Cliques*, The Problem With Cliques in Church, ¶1-2.

23. YouthMinistry.com. *7 Steps*, ¶1.

24. Miedema, *5 Facts*, ¶1-2.

25. Orgeron, *Complex PTSD*, ¶4.

26. Orgeron, ¶5-7.

27. Mnookin, *Child-Custody Adjudication*.

28. Robinson, *Remedying Our Foster*, 396.

29. Azzi-Lessing, *Hidden harms*, Bleak futures for those aging out, ¶2-3.

30. O'Harrow, *Young Victims*, ¶24.

31. Villimain, *Children of prostitutes*, ¶1.

32. Fang, et. al., *economic burden*, 156.

33. d2l, *Impact of Child*, The Economic Impact, ¶1-2.

34. d2l, The Social Impact, ¶2.

35. ISSTD, *What is dissociation?*, ¶3.

36. Grossman, *Giving Your Child*, ¶1.

37. Grossman.

38. Mykids Ventures Private Limited. *Why Is It*, How Can I As a Parent Improve My Listening Skills, ¶1.

39. Close, *Listening to Children*, 20.

40. Smalley, *28 Rules*.

41. Salim, *importance of giving*, ¶1.

42. St. John and Briel, *Student Voice*, Introduction, ¶2.

43. St. John and Briel, Benefits of Increasing Student Voice, ¶1.

44. Tucker, *Positive & Negative*, Ability to Handle Loss, ¶2.

45. Divecha, *What are*, ¶1.

46. Divecha, Building a positive school climate, ¶2.

47. Lesley University, *6 Ways.*, Identify 'gateway behaviors'.

48. Divecha, *What are*, Advancing social and emotional learning, ¶1.

49. Crisis Prevention Institute, *10 Ways.*

50. Harmon, *3 Ways.*

51. Ressler, *Church Cliques*, Recommendations, ¶1-2.

52. Hardin, *What Does*, How should Christians respond to bullying? 3. Even if you are wronged, respond in a Christ-like manner, ¶2.

53. Orgeron, *We Survived*, 51.

54. Orgeron, 51.

55. Orgeron, 53.

56. Orgeron, 56.

57. Frankel, *Giving Children*, 11.

58. Frankel, 11.

59. Orgeron, Milton & Pam, *Why World Needs*, ¶1.

60. Orgeron, *Finding Freedom*, 112.

61. Orgeron, *Types, Causes, Consequences*, 72.

62. MFMER, *Klinefelter syndrome*, ¶1.

63. APA Dictionary of Psychology, *self-fulfilling prophecy.*

* * *

BIBLIOGRAPHY & RECOMMENDED RESOURCES

Allen, Jackie M. and Doris Rhea Coy. 2004. "Linking Spirituality and Violence Prevention in School Counseling." *Professional School Counseling* 7 (June): 351-355.

Allender, Dan B. 1990. *The Wounded Heart: Hope for Adult Victims of Childhood Sexual Abuse.* Colorado Springs: NavPress.

Alsgaard, Erik. n.d. "Bullying happens in church. Don't ignore it!" ResourceUMC.org. Accessed April 17, 2020. https://www.resourceumc.org/en/content/bullying-happens-in-church-dont-ignore-it.

American Professional Society on the Abuse of Children. 2018 (website). Accessed April 16, 2020. https://www.apsac.org/.

American Psychological Association (APA). 2020. "Bullying and School Climate." Accessed April 17, 2020. https://www.apa.org/advocacy/interpersonal-violence/bullying-school-climate.

APA Dictionary of Psychology. 2020. "self-fulfilling prophecy." Accessed April 26, 2020. https://dictionary.apa.org/self-fulfilling-prophecy.

Arterburn, Stephen. 1992. *Hand-Me-Down Genes and Second-Hand Emotions.* Nashville: Thomas Nelson.

Arterburn, Stephen, and Jack Felton. 1991/1992. *Faith That Hurts Faith That Heals: Understanding the Fine Line Between Healthy Faith and Spiritual Abuse.* Nashville: Thomas Nelson.

Azzi-Lessing, Lenette. 2016. "The hidden harms of the US foster-care system." The Conversation. Jan. 22, 2016. Accessed April 20, 2020. https://theconversation.com/the-hidden-harms-of-the-us-foster-care-system-49700.

Baldwin, Stanley C. 1989. *If I'm Created in God's Image, Why Does It Hurt to Look in the Mirror?: A True View of You.* Lynnwood, WA: Aglow.

Beattie, Melody. 1989. *Beyond Codependency: And Getting Better All the Time.* San Francisco: Harper & Row.

Beattie, Melody. 1987. *Codependent No More.* USA: Hazelden.

Beckelman, Laurie. 1978. Why the Cry of the Beaten Child Goes Unheard. *The New York Times.*, April 16, 1978. Accessed January 10, 2019. https://www.nytimes.com/1978/04/16/archives/why-the-cry-of-the-beaten-child-goes-unheard.html.

"Bullying in Schools: Guide for Teachers." n.d. Study.com. Accessed April 17, 2020. https://study.com/teach/bullying-in-schools.html.

Burton, Randy. n.d. "System is Failing Children." Justice for Children. Accessed April 14, 2020. https://justiceforchildren.org/about-us/system-is-failing-our-children/.

Carnes, Patrick. 1993. *A Gentle Path through the Twelve Steps (2nd ed.).* Minneapolis: CompCare.

Celebrate Recovery, a Christ-Centered 12 Step Program. 2018. (website). Accessed April 16, 2020. https://www.celebraterecovery.com/.

Chansky, Tamar E. 2020. *Freeing Your Child from Negative Thinking: Powerful, Practical Strategies to Build a Lifetime of Resilience, Flexibility, and Happiness.* 2nd ed. Boston, MA: Da Capo Lifelong Books.

Child Welfare Information Gateway. n.d. (website). Accessed April 16, 2020. https://www.childwelfare.gov/.

Child Welfare League of America. n.d. (website). Accessed April 16, 2020. https://www.cwla.org/.

Childhelp, Prevention and Treatment of Child Abuse. n.d. (website). Accessed April 16, 2020. https://www.childhelp.org/.

Children Without a Voice USA. 2019. (website). Accessed April 16, 2020. http://www.cwavusa.org/.

Children's Bureau Express (CBX). n.d. (website). Accessed April 16, 2020. https://cbexpress.acf.hhs.gov/.

Close, Nancy. 2002. *Listening to Children: Talking With Children About Difficult Issues.* Boston, MA: Allyn and Bacon.

Crisis Prevention Institute. 2020. "10 Ways to Help Reduce Bullying in Schools" (blog). Accessed April 23, 2020. https://www.crisisprevention.com/Blog/10-Ways-to-Help-Reduce-Bullying-in-Schools.

Dake, Joseph A., James H. Price, and Susan K. Telljohann. 2003. "The Nature and Extent of Bullying at School." *Journal of School Health* 73 (May): 173-180.

Darkness to Light. 2020. "The Impact of Child Sexual Abuse." Accessed April 16, 2020. https://www.d2l.org/the-issue/impact/.

Dent, Renuka. J., and, R. J. Sean Cameron. 2003. Developing Resilience in Children Who are in Public Care: The educational psychology perspective. *Educational Psychology in Practice, 19* (March): 3-19.

Divecha, Diana. 2019. "What Are the Best Ways to Prevent Bullying in Schools?" *Greater Good Magazine*, Oct. 29, 2019. Accessed April 22, 2020. https://greatergood.berkeley.edu/article/item/what_are_the_best_ways_to_prevent_bullying_in_schools

Dobson, James. 2018. "Sexual Abuse and Homosexuality." The Dobson Library. Accessed January 10, 2019. https://www.dobsonlibrary.com/resource/article/a911a4f3-eac9-4c04-807d-49e715440373.

Donovan, Mary E., and William P. Ryan. 1991. *Love Blocks: Breaking the Patterns That Undermine Relationships.* New York: Penguin.

Fang, Xiangming, Derek S. Brown, Curtis S. Florence, and James A. Mercy. 2012. "The economic burden of child maltreatment in the United States and implications for prevention." Child Abuse & Neglect, 36(2): 156-165.

Frank, Jan. 1995. A Door of Hope: Recognizing and Resolving the Pains of Your Past. San Bernardino, CA: Here's Life.

Frankel, Sam. 2018. "Giving Children a Voice: A Step-by-Step Guide to Promoting Child-Centred Practice." March 2018. Accessed April 30, 2020. http://www.jkp.com/jkpblog/wp-content/uploads/2018/03/Frankel-9781784505783.pdf

Gambill, Beck. 2016. "When Bullying Comes to Church." Christian and Missionary Alliance (blog). Accessed April 17, 2020. https://cmalliancekids.com/when-bullying-comes-to-church/.

Genesis Process. n.d.. (website). Accessed April 16, 2020. https://www.genesisprocess.org/.

Grossman, Richard. n.d.. "Giving Your Child 'voice': The 3 Rules of Parenting." The Natural Child Project. Accessed January 10, 2019. https://www.naturalchild.org/articles/guest/richard_grossman.html.

Hardin, Neal. 2018. "What Does the Bible Teach Us About Bullying." Accessed April 25, 2020. https://churchleaders.com/pastors/pastor-articles/334798-what-does-the-bible-teach-us-about-bullying-neal-hardin.html

Harmon, Matthew. 2020, "3 Ways to Handle False Teaching and False Teachers." Bible Study Tools (blog). Accessed April 25, 2020. https://www.biblestudytools.com/blogs/matthew-s-harmon/how-gospel-centered-churches-handle-false-teaching-and-false-teachers-titus-1-10-16.html

Hemfelt, Robert, Frank Minirth, and Paul Meier. 1989. *Love is a Choice: Recovery for Codependent Relationships.* Nashville: Thomas Nelson.

International Society for the Study of Trauma & Dissociation. 2020. "What is dissociation?" Dissociation FAQs. Accessed April 19, 2020. https://www.isst-d.org/resources/dissociation-faqs/.

Krueger, Joline G. 2018. "In custody case, children's voices go unheard." *Albuquerque Journal,* Jan. 15, 2018. Accessed Jan. 10, 2019. https://www.abqjournal.com/1119350/in-custody-case-childrens-voices-go-unheard.html.

LaHaye, Tim, and Beverly LaHaye. 2009. *The Act of Marriage: The Beauty of Sexual Love.* Grand Rapids: Zondervan.

Lesley University. n.d. "6 Ways Educators Can Prevent Bullying in Schools." Accessed April 23, 2020. https://lesley.edu/article/6-ways-educators-can-prevent-bullying-in-schools.

Martin, Gary. 2020. "Sticks and stones may break my bones." The Phrase Finder. Accessed April 13, 2020. https://www.phrases.org.uk/meanings/sticks-and-stones-may-break-my-bones.html.

Mayo Foundation for Medical Education and Research (MFMER). 1998-2020. *Diseases and conditions: Klinefelter syndrome: Definition.* Accessed May 2, 2020. https://www.mayoclinic.org/diseases-conditions/klinefelter-syndrome/symptoms-causes/syc-20353949.

McDonald, Trey. 2019. "Fighting the Cliques in Your Church." Ministry Impact Resources, October 10, 2019. Accessed April 17, 2020. https://ministry.acst.com/fighting-the-cliques-in-your-church/.

McGee, Robert S. 2003. *The Search for Significance: Seeing Your True Worth Through God's Eyes.* Nashville: Thomas Nelson.

McGee, Robert S., Jim Craddock, and Pat Springle. 1990. *Your Parents and You.* USA: Rapha & Word.

Mend Your Soul Life Coaching. 2019. (website). Accessed April 16, 2020. https://mendyoursoul.com/you-can-take-your-life-back.--discover-your-freedom--from-the-impact-of-relational-abuse..html.

Middleton-Moz, Jane, and Lorie L. Dwinell. 2010. *After the Tears: Helping Adult Children of Alcoholics Heal Their Childhood Trauma.* Deerfield Beach, FL: Health Communications.

Miedema, Rachel. 2016. "5 Facts on Bullying Youth Leaders Need to Know." The Youth Cartel (blog). November 16, 2016. Accessed April 18, 2020. https://theyouthcartel.com/5-facts-on-bullying-youth-leaders-need-to-know/.

Minirth, Frank, B., and Paul D. Meier. 2013. *Happiness is a Choice: New Ways to Enhance Joy and Meaning in Your Life.* Grand Rapids: Baker.

Mnookin, Robert H. 1975. "Child-Custody Adjudication: Judicial Functions in the Face of Indeterminacy." *Law and Contemporary Problems,* Summer 1975. Accessed April 20, 2020. https://scholarship.law.duke.edu/lcp/vol39/iss3/8/.

Mykids Ventures Private Limited. n.d. "Why Is It Important To Listen To Your Child." Accessed April 21, 2020. https://www.beingtheparent.com/why-is-it-important-to-listen-to-your-child/.

National Center for Missing & Exploited Children. 2020. (website). Accessed April 16, 2020. https://www.missingkids.org/.

National Center on Shaken Baby Syndrome. n.d. (website). Accessed April 16, 2020. https://www.dontshake.org/.

National Child Traumatic Stress Network. n.d.. (website). Accessed April 16, 2020. https://www.nctsn.org/.

National CASA/GAL Association for Children.. 2020. (website). Accessed April 16, 2020. https://nationalcasagal.org/.

National Sexual Violence Resource Center. 2018. (website). Accessed April 16, 2020. https://www.nsvrc.org/about/national-sexual-violence-resource-center.

National Suicide Prevention Lifeline (800-273-8255). n.d.. (website). Accessed April 16, 2020. https://suicidepreventionlifeline.org/.

O'Harrow, Robert., Jr. 1992. "Young Victims of Sex Abuse Go Unheard." *The Washington Post,* March 15, 1992. Accessed January 10, 2019. https://www.washingtonpost.com/archive/local/1992/03/15/young-victims-of-sex-abuse-go-unheard/259a6357-2b0d-429b-a3a6-3e86f2febdfa/?noredirect=on&utm_term=.71b7865dc1af.

Olweus Dan. 1994. "Annotation: Bullying at School: Basic Facts and Effects of a School Based Intervention Program." In: Huesmann L.R. (ed.) Aggressive Behavior. The Plenum Series in Social/Clinical Psychology. Springer, Boston, MA. Journal of Child Psychology and Psychiatry 35(7):1171-1190. Accessed April 17, 2020. https://www.researchgate.net/profile/Dan_Olweus/publication/15391812_Bullying_at_School_Basic_Facts_and_Effects_of_a_School_Based_Intervention_Program/links/59ddf4a3aca272204c2bca5d/Bullying-at-School-Basic-Facts-and-Effects-of-a-School-Based-Intervention-Program.pdf.

Omartian, Stormie. 1992. *A Step in the Right Direction: Your Guide to Inner Happiness.* Nashville: Thomas Nelson.

Orgeron, Milton J. and Pamela K. Orgeron. 2018. "Why the World Needs Revival and Spiritual Awakening, Part 1" (blog). ABC's Ministries. Jan. 22, 2018. Accessed May 3,

2020. https://abcsministries.wordpress.com/2018/01/22/ why-the-world-needs-revival-and-spiritual-awakening-part-1/.

Orgeron, Pamela K. 2016. *We Survived Sexual Abuse! You Can Too! Personal Stories of Sexual Abuse Survivors with Information about Sexual Abuse Prevention, Effects, and Recovery.* Madison, TN: ABC's Ministries.

Orgeron, Pamela. K. 2017. *Food as an Idol: Finding Freedom from Disordered Eating.* Nashville, TN: ABC's Ministries.

Orgeron, Pamela K. 2018. "Complex PTSD...No Easy Battle." ABC's Ministries (blog). June 24, 2018. Accessed April 20, 2020. https://abcsministries.wordpress.com/2018/06/24/ complex-ptsd-no-easy-battle/.

Orgeron, Pamela K. 2019. *Food as an Idol: The Types, Causes, Consequences, Conquering, and Prevention of Disordered Eating.* Nashville: ABC's Ministries.

Owens (aka, Orgeron), Pamela K. 2001. "Counseling Sexuality: A Christian Perspective." Unpublished manuscript. Morehead State University at Morehead, KY.

'Parents should learn to listen to their kids'. 2015. *The Times of India,* April 23. 2015. Accessed April 15, 2020. https://timesofindia. indiatimes.com/city/bhubaneswar/Parents-should-learn-to-listen-to-their-kids/articleshow/47020379.cms.

Pychyl, Timothy, A. 2010. Personality, Homework Behavior and Academic Performance: How does personality relate to homework and grades? *Psychology Today,* Jan. 18, 2010. Accessed April 15, 2020. https://www. psychologytoday.com/us/blog/dont-delay/201001/personality-homework-behavior-and-academic-performance.

Rainer, Thom, S. 2014. "Fourteen Symptoms of Toxic Church Leaders." (blog), Oct. 1, 2014. Accessed April 11, 2020. https://thomrainer.com/2014/10/fourteen-symptoms-toxic-church-leaders/.

RAINN (Rape, Abuse & Incest National Network). 2020. (website). Accessed April 16, 2020. https://www.rainn.org/.

Redleaf, Diane. 2019. "After the Hotline Call." *The Atlantic*, Jan. 27, 2019. Accessed April 15, 2020. https://www.theatlantic.com/

ideas/archive/2019/01/problem-child-protective-services/
580771/.

Ressler, Chad. n.d. "Church Cliques." Christian Apologetics &
Research Ministry. Accessed April 25, 2020. https://carm.org/
church-cliques

Robinson, Stacy. 1993. "Remedying Our Foster Care System:
Recognizing Children's Voices." *Family Law Quarterly* 27
(3): 395-415. Accessed April 14, 2020. www.jstor.org/stable/
25739947.

Salim, Ainee S. 2015. "The importance of giving students a voice."
The Express Tribune, Sept. 17, 2015. Accessed April 22,
2020. https://tribune.com.pk/story/958685/the-importance-
of-giving-students-a-voice/.

Sankaran, Vivek. 2019. "In Court, Children are Unseen and
Unheard." *Chronicle of Social Change*, Feb. 14, 2019. Accessed
April 14, 2020. https://chronicleofsocialchange.org/opinion/
in-court-children-are-too-often-unseen-and-unheard/33819.

Shaken Baby Alliance. 2017. (website). Accessed April 16, 2020.
https://www.shakenbaby.org/index.aspx.

Smalley, Michael, and Amy Smalley. 2006. "28 Rules for Resolving
Conflict with Your Children." Dec. 25, 2006. Accessed April
21, 2020. https://www.crosswalk.com/family/parenting/28-
rules-for-resolving-conflict-with-your-children-1459077.html

Springle, Pat. 1991. *Close Enough to Care: Helping a Friend or
Relative Conquer Codependency.* Houston & Dallas, Texas:
Rapha & Word.

Stanley, Charles F. 2005. *Our Unmet Needs.* Nashville: Thomas
Nelson.

St.John, Kendel, and Lori Briel. 2017. "Student Voice: A growing
movement within education that benefits students and teachers."
VCU Center on Transition Innovations. April 2017. Accessed
April 22, 2020. https://centerontransition.org/publications/
download.cfm?id=61.

St.John, Lanae. 2017. "Why raising children to be 'seen and not
heard' makes them targets for predators." Your Tango (blog).
May 5, 2017. Accessed April 13, 2020. https://www.yourtango.

com/2017302552/problem-children-being-seen-and-not-heard-it-makes-them-targets-sexual-predators.

Stonehouse, Catherine, and Scottie May. 2010. *Listening to Children on the Spiritual Journey: Guidance for Those Who Teach and Nurture*. Grand Rapids, MI: Baker.

Tucker, Kristine. 2018. "Positive & Negative Effects of Competition on Academic Achievement." June 25, 2018. Accessed April 22, 2020. https://www.theclassroom.com/positive-negative-effects-competition-academic-achievement-6928.html.

Tuten, Elizabeth. 2018. "Hurt Kids Hurt Kids: How One D.C. School is Attempting to Break the Bully Cycle." Communities In Schools (blog). Oct. 24, 2018. Accessed April 17, 2020. https://www.communitiesinschools.org/blog/2018/10/hurt-kids-hurt-kids-how-one-dc-school-attempting-break-bully-cycle/.

U. S. Department of Health and Human Services. n.d. "What is Cyberbullying." Accessed April 17, 2020. https://www.stopbullying.gov/cyberbullying/what-is-it.

Villemain, Matthew. 2015. "The children of prostitutes: The victims without a voice." *ckm! Centrum Kinderhandel Mensenhandel*, May 3, 2015. Accessed January 10, 2019. https://www.ckm-fier.nl/The-Children-of-Prostitutes-the-victims-without-a-voice.ashx.

Walker, Pete. 2013. *Complex PTSD: From surviving to thriving—A guide and map for recovering from childhood trauma*. USA: CreateSpace Independent Publishing.

Warren, Neil, C. 1997. *Finding Contentment*. Nashville: Thomas Nelson.

Weinschneider, Ely, and Alison Maloni. 2019. "A good parent is a parent who takes the time to listen to their children." *Thrive Global*, Feb. 27, 2019. Accessed April 15, 2020. https://thriveglobal.com/stories/a-good-parent-is-a-parent-who-takes-the-time-to-listen-to-their-children-by-dr-ely-weinschneider-and-alison-maloni/.

Whealin, Julia, and Erin Barnett. 2019. "Child Sexual Abuse." U.S. Department of Veterans Affairs, PTSD: National Center for

PTSD, October 14, 2019. Accessed May 6, 2020. https://www.ptsd.va.gov/professional/treat/type/sexual_abuse_child.asp.

"Why Is It Important To Listen To Your Child?" n.d.. Accessed April 15, 2020. https://www.beingtheparent.com/why-is-it-important-to-listen-to-your-child/.

Writing Explained. 2020. *What Does Children Should Be Seen and Not Heard Mean?* Accessed April 13, 2020. https://writingexplained.org/idiom-dictionary/children-should-be-seen-and-not-heard.

Youth Ministry. 2020. "7 Steps in Dealing with Cliques." Accessed April 18, 2020. https://youthministry.com/7-steps-in-dealing-with-cliques/#comments.

* * *

ABOUT THE AUTHOR

Pam Orgeron

Pamela K. Orgeron, M.A., Ed.S., BCCC, ACLC, formerly Pamela K. Owens (1960-) was born in Ashland, KY. In 1986 she received a B.A. degree in Journalism-Public Relations from Marshall University, Huntington, WV. Also in 1986 Ms. Owens moved to Nashville, TN where she spent over 8 years employed with the Jean and Alexander Heard Library, Vanderbilt University. Before moving back to Kentucky in 2000, she also worked for Harris Publishing and Thomas Nelson Publishers. Ms. Owens received both an M.A. (2003) and an Ed.S. (2009) degree in Adult & Higher Education, Counseling Specialization from Morehead State University, Morehead, KY. Ms. Owens moved back to Nashville in 2009. Since then she has received an Advanced Diploma in Biblical Counseling from Light University and became a Board Certified Christian Counselor and a Board Certified Advanced Christian Life Coach. In 2010 she married Milton J. Orgeron. She and Milton are General Partners in *ABC's* Ministries, and are members of Parkway Baptist Church, Goodlettsville, TN. Mrs. Orgeron also is a certified writer with the Institute of Children's Literature, West Redding, Connecticut. She also is a member of the American Association of Christian Counselors, the International Christian Coaching Association, and the Christian Association of Psychological Studies.

* * *

Pamela K. Orgeron, M.A., Ed.S., BCCC, ACLC
Christian Author, Counselor, & Life Coach
General Partner, ABC's Ministries

Contact Pam through the following:
https://www.facebook.com/AttnPamatABCsMinistries/
https://www.linkedin.com/in/pamela-orgeron-57873045/

For more information
about ABC's Ministries:
Visit the Website:
https://abcsministries.wordpress.com/

E-mail us at:
abcsministries@yahoo.com

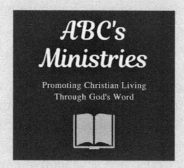

Lightning Source UK Ltd.
Milton Keynes UK
UKHW051828030820
367514UK00024B/445